Being Nude

Being Nude

THE SKIN OF IMAGES

Jean-Luc Nancy and Federico Ferrari

TRANSLATED BY ANNE O'BYRNE AND CARLIE ANGLEMIRE

Fordham University Press / *New York* / 2014

This work has been published with the assistance of the French Ministry of Culture—National Center for the Book.

Ouvrage publié avec le concours du Ministère français chargé de la culture—Centre National du Livre.

Library of Congress Cataloging-in-Publication Data

Ferrari, Federico, author.
   [Nus sommes. English]
   Being nude : the skin of images / Jean-Luc Nancy and Federico Ferrari ; translated by Anne O'Byrne and Carlie Anglemire.
      pages   cm
   Summary: "26 reflections on nude images from the history of Western art including Rembrandt, Goya, David Hockney and Nan Golden. The authors, both philosophers, develop an approach to the nude that involves shedding preconceived concepts and exposing ourselves to the fleeting sense that passes over the surface of the nude's skin and over the surface of the image"— Provided by publisher.
   Includes bibliographical references.
   ISBN 978-0-8232-5620-4 (hardback) — ISBN 978-0-8232-5621-1 (paper)
   1. Nude in art.   2. Nudity—Psychological aspects.   3. Aesthetics.
I. Nancy, Jean-Luc, author.   II. O'Byrne, Anne E. (Anne Elizabeth), 1966– translator.   III. Title.

   N7572.F47213 2014
   704.9'421—dc23
      2013049272

Printed in the United States of America
16 15 14   5 4 3 2 1

First edition

Contents

Preamble / 1

A Acephalous / 7

B Bathsheba / 11

C Caress / 17

D Disfiguration / 23

E Equivocal / 27

F Fenestration / 31

G Goya / 35

H Humus / 41

I Incarnate / 47

J Joker / 51

K Khaos / 55

L Lumbar / 59

M Model / 63

N Nimbus / 67

O Optic / 71

P Presence / 75

Q Quodlibet / 79

R Resurrection / 85

S Scopophilia / 87

T Trans / 91

U Use / 97

V Veritas / 103

W We / 109

X X / 113

Y Y / 117

Z Zero / 121

Illustration Sources and Credits / 123
Notes / 125

Nus sommes

Giacometti began a poem like this, taking pleasure in hearing *nus* (naked) as he pronounced it with his Italian accent: *nous* (we). He wrote:

nus sommes	we are naked
nus lisses	nude smooth
la si do	so la do
ré mi	mi re
et puis	and then
tire	go
gris	gray

We [*nous*]. Naked [*nus*]. We are naked [*nous sommes nus*]. This does not make nudity a being. It only makes nudes of us: exposed, fragile, thin bodies lying beside each other, turned toward one another, presenting the images that they are, images of a presence without secrets and without reason. The smooth surface of our images, of our skin, whose satiny or withered texture dissolves into musical notes, smooth, so la do, before the line in a gray drawing has been drawn.

SOURCE: Alberto Giacometti, *Écrits*. Edited by Michel Leiris et Jacques Dupin (Paris, Hermann, 1990) 139.

Preamble

Preamble: before ambling off or taking a walk, for example, through a picture gallery . . . This one offers twenty-six pictures, paintings or photographs chosen for no reason but the arbitrariness and chance of our two tastes and interests. This arbitrariness exposes us in a certain nudity. We have not clothed ourselves in knowledge or philosophy. We have no pretext or end to motivate a particular approach. In fact, it's not even really an approach, just a walk, a flaneur's wandering, which doesn't have to justify itself.

Our interest in the nude is the most widely shared thing in the world—at least, in the world of Western art, since other regions and periods of art have made nudity serve other interests. In fact, one might say that everywhere else, nudity seems to be understood in erotic and/or sacred terms, whereas the Western nude seems to be exposed for its own sake and to offer an interest in itself that is not related to the ends of knowledge or pleasure. Undoubtedly, it always seems ready to be turned toward something true or an experience of jouissance. But it nevertheless remains suspended, withdrawn, and undecidable. We are likewise exposed, without theory or art history, in our own encounters with the figures or singular moments of this nude that interests art for its own sake. Of course, it always also awakens some movement of curiosity or desire, but is never reduced to it. This movement is so obvious and conventional that it is clear that the nude wants something else—or that it wants nothing but to be nude.

What guided us both, each in our own way, is this sort of presence that is both filled with and stripped of itself, a withholding of complete exposition, the mingling of modesty and audacity in an appearing that assumes or consumes being. It is not really being, but rather a flash, not permanence, but the instantaneousness of what cannot take root. It is not a sense to be discerned or deciphered behind all the signs and strokes, but above all something true right at the skin.

Something true right at the skin, skin as truth: neither the beyond-the-skin sought by desire, nor the underside that science aims for, nor the spiritual secret of flesh revealed. For us, the nude is neither erotic nor anatomical nor authentic. It remains on the edge of or beyond these three postulations. The truth right at the skin is only true in being exposed, in being offered without reserve but also without revelation. After all, what the nude reveals is that there is nothing to be revealed, or that there is nothing other than revelation itself, the revealing and what can be revealed, both at once. It doesn't have the power to lay bare; that is to say, it is naked only in this very narrow place—the skin—and for this very brief time.

If a nude is not relentlessly its own stripping bare, if it is not each time its appearance and the simultaneous fragility, modesty, and flash of this appearing that makes nothing appear other than appearing itself, then it is not "nude" but "nudity," a spectacle for the science of observation or lascivious manipulation.

That is why the image is its element, and its skin is always the skin of an image. What renders itself naked makes itself an image, pure exposition. It is no accident, then, nor a matter of objective or sensual curiosity, that the image devotes itself to the nude. The image of the nude replays its own nudity each time; it plays its own skin of the image: the complete presentation there in the foreground, on the only plane of the image, of what has precisely no other plane, no dissimulated depth, and no secret. The secret is on the skin (the secret and the sacred). Painting, drawing or photographing the nude always poses the same challenge: how to represent the unrepresentable fugacity of stripping bare, the instant modesty that comes to conceal revelation, and the indecency that comes to reveal the evasion.

The one and the other take turns exposing just this: here is a subject in the strict sense of the word, *sub-jectum*: there is nothing beneath it, and it no longer hides anything else. It rests on itself, and this "self" is the skin, the thinness of skin and its flesh color. What painting paints when it colors itself with "flesh" and what the photo captures when it takes a "body" is the trans-parency that plays on the skin, or that makes skin. This is an appearing that makes nothing appear, a luminosity that sheds light on itself alone, a diaphanous touch that allows one to make out nothing but its touch itself.

Today nudity has become a relentless motif of thought; perhaps it goes back to Nietzsche, the first contemporary thinker to scoff at Europeans in their "moral clothing," unable to get undressed without shame.[1] Perhaps it goes back much further, to those Greek statues whose nudity seems to us to have been divinity itself and whose artful nudity undoubtedly still retains a memory mixed with Christian anxiety about flesh, as well as the sense of an exposition that is both fragile and precious. These three tonalities of the nude—the divine nude, naked sin, and naked skin—occupy thought today in many different ways, and Levi-Strauss's title *L'homme nu* can serve as an emblem for this thought. The preoccupation occurs in different registers, from the horror of bodies thrown onto the charnel heap to the desperate desire to make bodies their own icons, and it always leads us back in the direction of stripping bare and coming undone. This ambiguous proximity is also an opportunity for thought, if, for thought, it is a matter above all else of remaining stripped bare of all received meaning and figures that have already been traced. The nudes of painters and photographers expose this bareness and suspense on the edge of a sense that is always nascent, always fleeting, on the surface of the skin, and on the surface of the image.

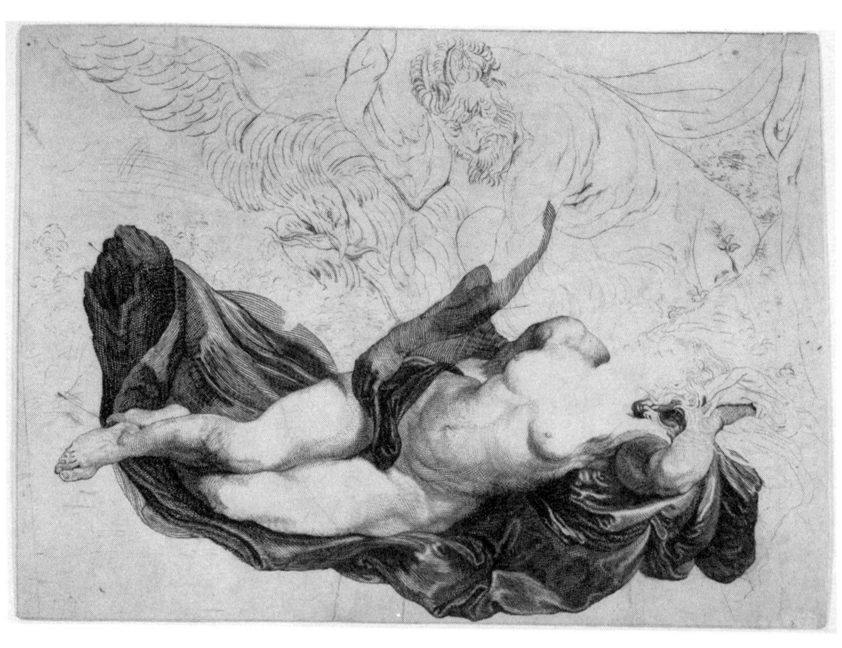

Acephalous

It's not just an unfinished drawing (in fact, it's the first state of a work). The fact that it is unfinished reveals something about the intention or the scene. If Antiope's face does not appear, it is because it is dispensable in the eyes of Zeus. His gaze is concentrated on the body. Transformed into a satyr, the god, a woman-chaser, covets a naked body, its belly, thighs, and breasts. Nudity is the prey here, and the face does not belong to it, because the face would demand something else from the satyr, something other than to be grabbed and made the recipient of his cum. The myth of Antiope is the story of a rape. But when gods assault mortals it often goes more or less like this: they want to fuck only the skin and the womb. This is how it was for Leda, Danae, Io, even for Europa—the bull carried her off without looking at her. They want a naked body, and that is what they take, with no concern for anything else. Here the hand of god is going to raise the veil that still, though only barely, covers the place he will penetrate. But already, as it falls, the veil takes on the shape of a phallus, of a prick coming to strike her in her sex.

(This engraving imitates a Van Dyck painting in which nothing is left unfinished. A comparison of the veils in the two images, as well as of the faces of the satyr, shows how much van der Steen wanted to emphasize the element of phallic violence.)

Brute and brutal desire reduces its object to a body without a head, and reduces this body to the crotch where desire wants to come. In the coupling of gods and mortals, it is always a matter of insemination, and there are always children as a result. In this case the children will be Amphion and Zethos.

But brute desire is not necessarily brutal. His lust can have all the violence of his turmoil. The naked body that throws him into turmoil for him signifies grabbing, thrusting, and pouring forth. This body is neither to be looked at nor listened to. It is to be handled, invaded, and inundated. It also has its head removed. Without a face, the body comes apart completely. Its nudity is a multiplicity of approaches and touches. This skin no longer holds together a unity: it becomes the occasion for the agitation to which it is offered: breasts to be grabbed, buttocks to be kneaded, thighs to be opened. At each point, there is a point to arouse, a tension to irritate. This nudity no longer consists of being undressed. It consists of being stretched and spread out, decapitated because separated from a center and a government.

The one who comes to take it in order to stir up his comings and goings does not dominate it: no one governs it any more. Both of them lose their heads. The one who takes also loses himself in the taking. He too is left naked: everything is thrown into his prick. The piece of cloth in the shape of a phallus no longer hides anything: it really is a penis with its naked shaft; it is the textile of the naked in its erectile texture. All the folds and unfoldings of the veil that billow beneath Antiope, all the learned study of draping and crumpling, all the palpable stretching and turning, is no longer either cloth or curtains but is really the effervescent foam that becomes the soul and therefore the form of the naked body itself.

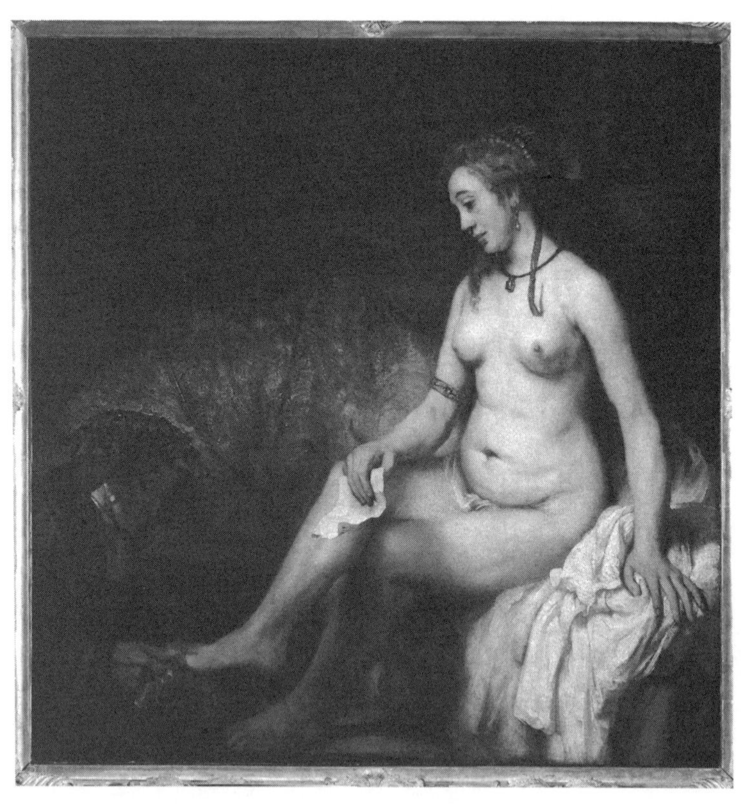

Bathsheba

In *The Nude: A Study in Ideal Form*, Kenneth Clark, following Erwin Panofsky, sets out the essential elements of a theory of the nude that is still very influential today among both art historians and experts in aesthetics.[2] According to this discourse, the nude constitutes the artistic–metaphysical genre par excellence. Insofar as it is abstracted from the dimension of the particular and the proper, the nude is the manifestation of something fixed, immobile, and timeless: beauty. Since it first appeared, the representation of the nude has therefore responded to one question: "What is man, in general?"[3] It is precisely because of its obstinate will to give a visible form to the human that the nude is the distinctive sign of Western society and the millenarian metaphysics that goes in search of a sensible image of the ideal. Greek statues are the most sophisticated example of this, since they are the tangible sign of the power of a people and a culture capable of extracting from brute, formless matter the abstract ideal of a humanity finally made accessible to the senses. The nude therefore represents not a body but an idea: the idea of man. It is not the demonstration of what "Man" is; it is "Man" himself, definitively exposed to a gaze with no vanishing lines, a gaze that is immobilized before the fixity and eternity of its essence.

11

But what is man? And what is man in general? Can we really think that "Nude" is the name that defines the humanity and essence of Man? Or do we have to start thinking that the "nude"—the "nude" that appeared with modernity and perhaps even earlier, in one type of Christian Renaissance art or another—is exactly this absence of name that only a proper name can inhabit? For us moderns, the Nude in itself does not exist. It has disappeared forever. The Nude met its end with the end of all humanism, that is, the end of all visions of the world that insisted that there was an evident universal essence of man. Man is not evident, not even in the nude. This is what modern art shows us.

Bathsheba is naked, immobile and sculptural, in an "absolute being-in-the-self" that is at the same time an absolute being-outside-the-self.[4] Bathsheba is silent: she is *infans*, wordless. Her gaze is lost in reading the letter from David. The language is indecipherable and leaves Bathsheba even more naked and disarmed: she is *ek-static*, outside herself, in a state of utter disorientation. Her body is in the gaze of another and in the written words that draw her beyond herself, into the world. The world of sense is suspended. Yet what remains is not the insignificance of pain or the hyper-significance of a model of humanity. What remains is the significance of her naked body and of a gaze that eludes every system of signs. The naked body and the gaze (of the nude and of the spectator) exceed the system of possible signification and establish a space with uncertain limits, in which the singular generality of an existence and the sense that it carries in itself suddenly appear.

In fact, sense doesn't really emerge, since it is already completely on the surface, on the surface of the body and on the surface of the painting over which the gaze passes. The nude is the surface of sense and as such it is neither the signifier nor the signified: it is pure signification, and the first exposition. The nude, nudity, and flesh melt into one another and/or oscillate in a balancing movement with no apparent resolution. The naked body of Bathsheba is a body of jouissance and suffering, but it is also a body completely exposed, outside itself on the liminal edge of its skin. The oil of the paint is the liminal layer of her flesh, but it is also the touch that gives pleasure on the surface of the body.

Unlike the formal model which inspired Rembrandt (an engraving by Perrier that reproduces an ancient Roman bas-relief showing a woman bathing with her servant), Bathsheba is naked, completely naked and completely detached from her historical context and from the hieratic, authoritative character of a biblical figure. And it is precisely nudity, the stripping bare of all models, that creates the *Heimatlosigkeit* that differentiates her from classical iconology and projects her not into the atemporality of a mythical dimension but into the new dimension of an unprecedented singularity.

By means of the singularity of its shape and its non-ideality, Bathsheba's body is the emblem of nudity itself, of the nudity of the moderns. The naked body is life-size. A little red velvet ribbon that hangs down from her hair and stands out against the dark colors all around her makes the whole painting vibrate and draws attention to her breasts. The left breast is slightly deformed: it's probably a tumor—the evil that insinuates itself into her body—an imperfection that makes her nudity even more singular. And it is exactly this absolute singularity, this unrepeatability in which evil disfigures beauty, that causes her nakedness to belong not to the order of (in)sensible sense but to the order of significance. Every sign effectively dissolves in repetition. Her nakedness is unrepeatable. Far from being a model, a definite and definitive essence, her nudity—like all nudities since, but also like many that came before—is the opening of an endless interrogation. In the end, the nude asks again: What is man in general? But only a singular name succeeds, time after time, in forming a feasible response in the face of the reiterated question. There is no response to the letter that Bathsheba holds in her hand and that asks to be deciphered, to receive a sense and an unequivocal response: words fail her. All that remains is the nudity of a wounded and disoriented woman, which becomes the crisis of every "metaphysics" of the sign, every will to hyper-signification, classification, systematization, granting of sense, and manifestation of essence. The question gets lost in the singularity of the flesh. It is the very essence of the nude that is lost. Short of and beyond every essence there remains the immanence of a body, its being there with no answers, totally exposed, and with no protection.

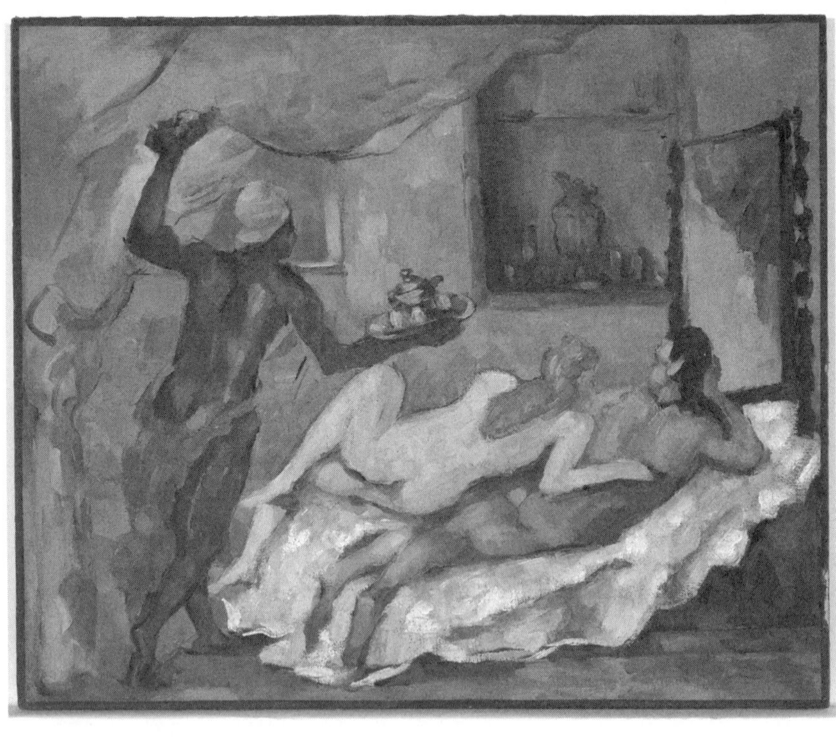

Caress

Is desire always in play in the representation of the nude? We may think so, but we cannot be sure. There are nudes that suspend desire, subordinating it to a presentation of forms that are not meant to be desired because they are content with taking pleasure in themselves, or with being their own desire and pleasure. These nudes, such as Titian's *Venus of Urbino*, Picasso's *Les Demoiselles d'Avignon* (and perhaps most of his nudes), and even, though in a different way, Modigliani's nudes are all sated. (Perhaps there are satisfied nudes, nudes of desire, and nudes of suffering, and maybe it is not always possible to impose just one of these categories on a given image.)

Desire can form the subject or the object of a representation, but this does not prevent it being both at the same time. It is the subject when a painting shows what a subject desires and that the subject desires it (it does not matter whether the subject is the painter or the spectator). It is the object when the painting shows desire at work. In Cézanne's *Afternoon in Naples*,[5] the two possibilities are conjoined. On the one hand, the scene that is shown is a scene of desire; on the other, the scene of monstration, or the showing scene, if one can put it that way, is the scene of the desire to see, to share or to touch the desire that is shown. This is because

17

what is shown, what both proposes and imposes itself, is the caress of two bodies toward which we advance through an entrance created by the lifting of a curtain (an anachronistic reference to an ancient pictorial topos) and by the movement of a servant who leads us in behind the couple, catching them in a caress. (Can a caress be seen, other than by surprise?) What is shown is the great flash of lightning, the white lightning of the woman's body stretched against the man's brown body, with an arm around him. One body is lying on top of the other, but as if lightly elevated above it, posing rather than posed, the whole in a fragile equilibrium. They are lying down but also suspended, capable of slipping or of a sort of leap, which the woman's left leg appears ready to make. The painting's lack of depth suggests that the woman's knee is touching the black arm of the servant, whose legs appear also to touch the woman's feet. Everything here touches and transmits the contact or contagion of desire and its arousal and satisfaction, its light touch and embrace, which is not, however, an interlacing. It is a light touch, with barely any pressure. It is the impression of skin against skin, right next to the skin. Nudity of desire, and therefore fragile nudity, which tastes suspense and indecision rather than enjoying possession. The naked bodies, supported and left in languorous expectation or repose, are reprised in the double gesture above them of the lifting of the curtain and the carrying and presenting of the tray bearing a discretely erectile teapot. What does it contain? A thirst-quenching beverage or a stimulating philter? Whatever it is, this is what, held in the air, occupies the center of the composition. This is what combines in the middle of the painting an aerial suspension and the promise of flowing. It is held and held out at the extremity of an élan that opens and approaches, an eruption of red and black with a golden head scarf, an almost naked body that comes, in its obscure presence, to share and multiply the caressing complicity. (Isn't a caress complicity in the first place?)

But there is yet another turn in this representation—there is, precisely, another presentation. (One is tempted to say: there is obviously another presentation, because all presentations call for their redoubling, even their excess. And this is so for nudity more than for any other presentation.)

This additional turn is given by the mirror (obviously!). We see only the reflection of the sheet in it—as well as, though very blurred and indistinct, the reflection of the black woman, a counterpoint to the white sheet. The undone sheet, spread out, signifies the love made on or beneath it, the love whose naked place this is. It signifies the nakedness of stripping lovers, like a veil falling from their exposed bodies as they undress and lie down, mingling in a warm, crumpling caress.

The reflected sheet falls along the vertical line of the mirror like a chute of water that goes on, passing beneath the frame of the mirror, continuing to froth in the eddies of the real sheet, flowing to the bottom of the painting, a stream that carries the bodies and bathes them, or that flows from them. (That this is about flowing, and flowing out, is suggested by the teapot as well as by the ewer in the niche, which reinterprets the theme of the vase with a generous mouth, which perhaps plays at being feminine, as the teapot plays at being masculine.) But if all we see in the mirror is this reflection, the two women must also see the reflection of the scene of which they are a part. The man turns his gaze toward the window, where the light of the sun reprises the golden tint of the lover's body. The women's gazes intercept each other in the front of the scene, which we see only from the back. From our position, we are led to believe that the mirror reflects their frontal nudity, their breasts and stomachs. It reflects the man's nudity, too, his relaxed penis, the fragile nudity of what has poured out.

All of the gazes—theirs and ours—are organized and captivated by this "before" that is turned toward the mirror or toward the sky and placed under the sign of the "after" (in front of / behind, in terms of space as well as time.) This is because the caress, during this moment of rest, already wants to begin again. It is content with its own spectacle and calls for its resumption, a fervor that is always renewed, just as naked bodies are always offered anew and always renew an infinite desire.

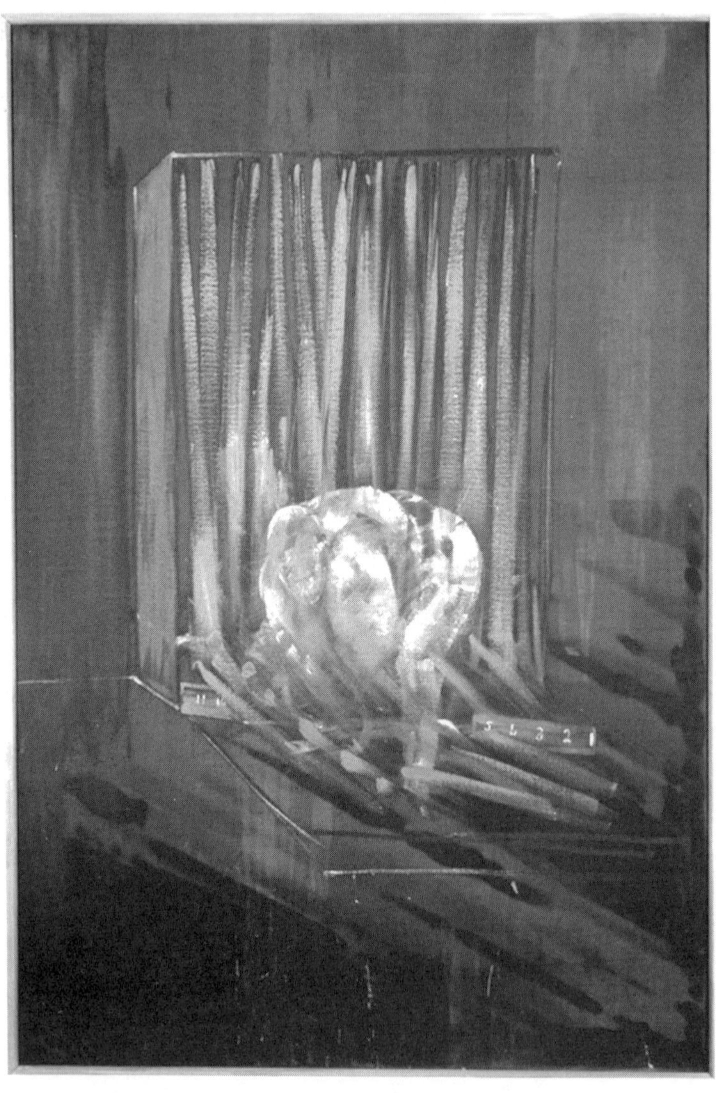

Disfiguration

In *Animal Locomotion*,[6] Eadweard Muybridge tried to arrest movement, to freeze a figure in motion, and afterward to bring it back to life through a succession of photograms. His sequences introduce—possibly for the first time in the history of all figurative art (including, therefore, photography)—time as a central element of representation. His nudes and plates of animal subjects consequently take on their true meaning only in a sequence, or, in a certain way, in a "chrono-photography." (Étienne-Jules Marey, who coined this word, was at the time one of the masters of this technique.) Thanks to Muybridge's work, the necessity of confronting the enigmatic relation that exists between figure and time, that is, the problem of a figure's movement and the way in which it is in motion, becomes fundamental and evident.

Already in Degas—who for a long time studied the work of this English photographer, his contemporary, in order to depict animals in motion at the center of his canvases— this problem appears absolutely modern and becomes the very heart of Modernity. Obviously, Futurism and Cubism realize its innovative elements and its most spectacular potentialities by working them out in infinite variations, but probably only with Bacon, in the domain of painting, was Muybridge's heritage really taken up, thought all the way through, and thereby reinvented.

Study for a Nude (1951) is one of Bacon's first nudes, and the indebtedness to Muybridge is immediately evident. The numbers that appear to the right of the figure are a reference to the numbering of Muybridge's photographs. Even the stage on which Muybridge's subjects usually move is partially retained, though it becomes a "theatrical cage," a black theater box in which the figure is about to dissolve. It is as if in moving the figure has been dissociated from itself, leaving only a trace of itself at each point in the space traversed. The figure is thus reduced, to put it as Bacon does, to a "trace of human presence," as if human presence always gives itself only as a trace or a collection of traces. For Bacon, it is no longer possible—by contrast to Muybridge—to put the figure in focus, to freeze it in motion. Liberated from cognitive or illustrative obligations, it moves within the picture space. There is no longer any need for a sequence (although we know that Bacon was also attracted by that possibility) to set it in motion, because the figure itself is movement. Muybridge's gesture is reversed: the numbers behind the figure are written backward. Bacon's painting is figurative insofar as it shows the movement that a body completes in order to become a figure. His use of color, the black of the ink into which the body seems to disappear, shows the research, the study, through which a naked body, in movement, succeeds in shattering the clichés of the Human Figure and exposes it to time, to birth and death, which come up so often—almost obsessively—in interviews with Bacon and in his work.

Bacon's painting is this infinite study, this repeated and never finished attempt to get the naked to show itself, to get one who is naked (a nude) to give itself as a figure. For Bacon, it is really the material of the nude—of the body, which is no more human than animal—that, more forcefully than any other subject, allows the disfiguring of figuration in order to make a figure and its movement appear. The pictorial gesture is skinned, stripped of all narrative, anatomical, classificatory, semantic, symbolic, or sanctifying intent. What appears is the simple presence of the real, its figural side: the nudity of a body. As Michel Leiris rightly writes, what appears is therefore art "stripped of all meaning beyond its own practice." This is the nudity of an art in which the true nature of all realist art emerges: the real is never a given; the real is realized. Painting is precisely the praxis at the heart of which the real realizes itself by becoming a figure exposed to time. And because of this exposure to the excesses of time, each figure—above all the nude figure, which is, of course, stripped of any ornamentation that could tie it to a particular temporality—is always in the process of disfiguring itself. The restlessness of time sets atremble the immobility that reigns in the mirror of the representation and propagates movement there. After this shock, after this rupture of spatiotemporal continuity, one can use the term *figure* only for this form (of life) that, stripped of everything, accepts the suspension of its proper fixity, its impassibility, and exposes itself to the continual disfiguration of itself, to the continual exceeding of the body in relation to the self that is the body's self. Only then can the act and the naked body become figure and realize themselves. They become an existence, a being-always-outside-of-itself, on the surface of the canvas, right at the skin.

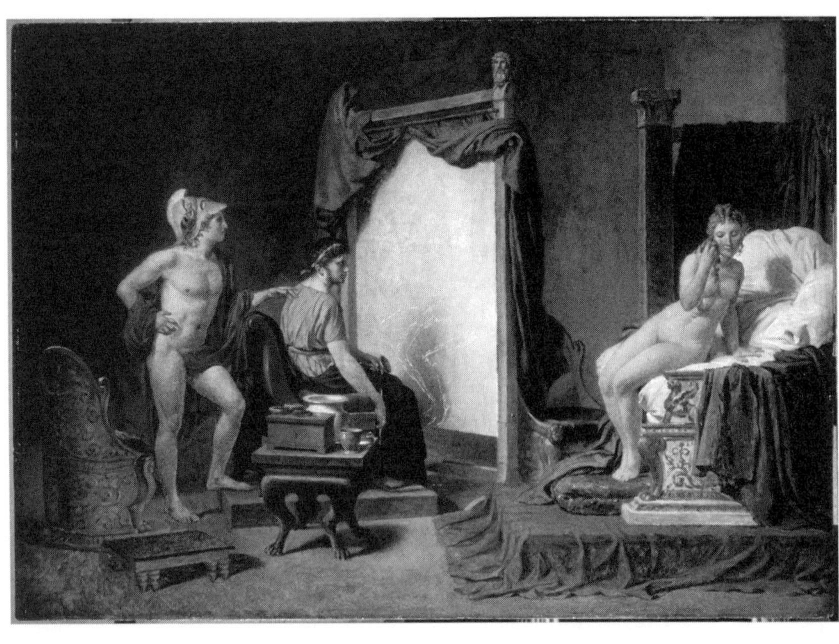

Equivocal

Alexander had his mistress Campaspe painted by the great painter Apelles, who was his official painter and the only one he allowed to do his portrait. Alexander wanted Campaspe naked *ob admirationem formae* ("in admiration of her beauty"), according to Pliny. While working, Apelles fell in love with her. The king noticed and offered his mistress to the painter. The scene was painted several times, but David represents it in a unique way. In lieu of a grouped scene, as in other works, he arranges it on a wide scale, so that the three people can be clearly seen. The two men, one behind the other, are turned toward the woman, who is at a distance from them. Her nudity is exposed to them, and out of modesty, though without being frightened, she makes a vague gesture of reserve. But for those who know the story, her embarrassment or her coquetry could both flatter her master while dissimulating her deception and also intensify her lover's desire while reassuring him of her mastery of the game. Campaspe's nudity, exposed as the truth of her beauty, is therefore the place of and what is at stake in an imbroglio of desire: both Alexander's desire and Apelles's are satisfied and frustrated. Alexander desires the image—desire for mastery, for supreme appropriation of this body that has already been possessed—although it has already been stolen from him. Apelles desires the body—which he also already possesses, even if he's only gripped it with his eyes—but he can only have the image (and the time to execute it).

Along with Campaspe's gestures of modesty, the carefully chosen décor tells us everything about the duplicity of nudity. This décor consists of nothing but the bed, whose white sheets are set off by black curtains. It is not only décor, a frame for presentation, but it is the painter's bed (as if one is meant to believe that Apelles sleeps in his studio . . . which he must in fact do when the king is not there). The modesty itself is ambiguous, because if Campaspe seems to make a vague gesture to cover herself with her hair, she covers nothing, neither her breasts nor her belly. The latter especially, more than any other part of her body, is the part most open to the painter's gaze. Elevated by the bed, this belly is presented at the same height as the bellies of the two men: they are aligned parallel to the axis of their gazes, which is also the axis along which the painting is carried out.

This, however, has only just begun. Unlike more than one predecessor who depicted the canvas covered with Campaspe's bust, David gives us only the lines of the beginning of a sketch, from the legs up to the stomach, which is still invisible. And on these indistinct lines falls the painter's shadow, at once hiding and highlighting them. Otherwise, the canvas is bare. (We know that David did not finish his painting: would he have then filled out Apelles's? . . .) The background color is reprised in certain parts of the bodies. The bare canvas is like the painting of the naked woman, though it is an expression rather than a representation of it, giving nudity a triple value: of exposition, stretched out, taut, offered to the paintbrush; of maneuverability and malleability, in the sense that the body the painter wants to give himself will come onto the canvas; and of distancing, insofar as the canvas also serves as a screen between the woman and the two men. (Screen or diversion: everything is set up as though there were two axes of the men's gazes, making them cross-eyed: the first is the axis of their gaze at the woman, the second of their gaze at her portrait. (In addition, the canvas is presented as a stage; a double black curtain is raised on it.)

That is not all. Nudity plays an even more restricted role here. Already at first glance, Alexander's naked body imposes itself, highlighted by the loose folds of royal purple cloth and the general's helmet. The master exhibits himself naked, facing his naked mistress: this display asserts his desire, is a reminder of possession, and highlights their symmetry and, in a certain way, their rivalry. Alexander's body, as the virile version of fine, sculpted form, does not cede anything to Campaspe's. At this point, the gaze of the spectator finds itself attracted to the painting's two extremities: toward one sex or the other. History (or legend? It doesn't matter here) would have it that Alexander was bisexual. We know how important the nude was to David, since he even produced a manuscript on it; this painting could in turn authorize an analysis in terms of bisexuality or homosexuality. So could the detail of Alexander's hand touching the painter's shoulder. However, one need only analyze the painting: nudity is clearly doubled, whether in heterosexual or homosexual fashion. But isn't this inherent in nudity in general? Is there isolated nudity? Isn't all nudity facing itself or facing another? Isn't nudity first of all a "facing?" Though it is one that never has a vis–à–vis, because the nude does not look. It is looked at, and also looks at itself. That is why the canvas is empty and bare: it is painting facing itself—like a great desire stretched out. The canvas is the one with an erection: look at the phallic summit at the height of the frame closest to us. The post of the bed nearby, crowned with a flared capital, is its counterpart.

Nudity is not a being. It is not even a quality. It is always a relation, several simultaneous relations, with others, with the self, with an image, and with the absence of an image.

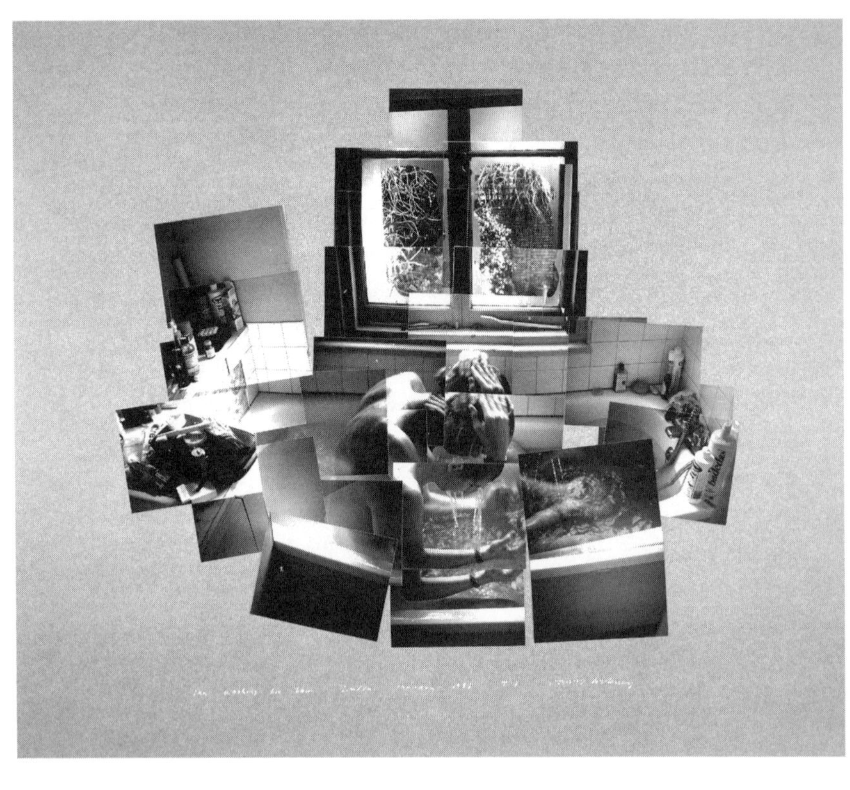

Fenestration

The history of Western art over the last five hundred years, which is also the history of the nude as a pictorial genre, appears in many regards as the repeated attempt of a furtive glance—peering through a window (as in Renaissance art, for example) or leaning over the lens of a camera obscura (as in seventeenth-century Dutch art)—to grasp a subject who is more or less aware of being observed. For this broad and heterogeneous tradition, the artist is the one who places himself in front of the window of the representation and fixes the time-space of the subject in the same frame. But if in painting and sculpture, on the one hand, the intervention of the "hand" of the artist is capable of introducing a time lag and a proliferation of spatial and temporal planes, in photography, on the other, the reduction to a single spatiotemporal dimension becomes inevitable. Normally, photography arrests time. It attests to the presence of an object by making it "instantaneous." There is no longer any trace of the "hand" and its movements in the pictorial space, movements that are all at different moments and are distant from one another.

According to a hypothesis about Western representation[7]—which was shared by the artist David Hockney, according to many of his writings—the subject of photography, the nude in particular, becomes an object on which a spatiotemporal unity is imposed. Its only space-time becomes the space-time of the viewer, the eye of the one who is looking through the "window." Its existence is gathered into the unity of a gaze and is thereby expropriated from its corporeal presence, from the fragmentation of sensations and heterogeneous temporalities that the body represents for the subject. As Barthes writes in *Camera Lucida: Reflections on Photography*, "photography is the advent of myself as other."[8] My body becomes an object that I can observe, an inanimate clone. Often, the photographic nude is therefore one-dimensional. In photographic instantaneity it loses the capacity for motion in time and space that makes it living. It is almost always like this. But not always. Sometimes, the "window" of the gaze explodes and the body takes on a different vitality.

Ian Washing His Hair (1983) is one of Hockney's most famous photographic collages. His first composition of this sort dates from 1982 and seems immediately to be an attempt to extend the pictorial gesture to the technique of photography. Hockney tries to free photography from its "punctual" or "instantaneous" character in order to give it the movement of a drawing. The idea is to create visions by means of sequences: not an ensemble of points but the continuity—albeit broken continuity—of a line; not the trace of a body but the thing that is traced and thereby given life. Vision must try to render the fragmentary character of the sensations that a body gives and receives within a determinate space. In *Ian*, the subject is inside the camera obscura and the artist is not in front of the window of vision. He too is inside the image; he too sees and is observed from the window. The "open window," in perspective, signals the homogeneity and coherence of the space of representation that Leon Battista Alberti had already discussed in his *On Painting*. Here it is visible in the image, but reduced to a series of fragments.[9] The window, the place of vision, has become an object of representation. However, Hockney does not limit himself to constructing a meta-image, to showing the access through which vision is given—a gesture that is common to much of contemporary art. He places himself in the image and tries to render its internal fragmentation, the internal fracture that characterizes access (insofar as there is no [point] outside of access from which one could observe access—this is the great illusion of metaphysical art). As a result, it is not only a presentation of presentation, a vision of vision, but also the originary fragmentation that all vision is in itself, in its always being outside itself, exposed to the gaze of the other. This "first" alterity is the singular body of all "nudity." The *Ur-teilung* of the naked vision of a naked body. It is the originary partition within which the space of representation opens, the division of the subject that precedes all identity.

Hockney does not try to fix the naked body in a single figure. He does not try to give it an identity, but rather contents himself with letting it move in the representation. Ian's hands move rhythmically. Although objects can still be brought into focus and can stay still—even though they are caught in originary division—the naked body and the hand that tries to touch it cannot be fixed in one point of the space because they are an inexhaustible source of spacing.

The parties enter into relation with one another without giving birth to any unity, not even the unity of the body. The image does not close over; it fails to come to a standstill or to insist on a particular whole. The eye is set in motion. The nude is the mobility of the eye, its motion and emotion. One can only follow it and render its rhythm.

The art of the rhythm and time of exposition. The double exposition of the window-diaphragm of the camera obscura: the exposition of the existence of a naked vision, and the exposition to vision of naked, everyday existence—*Ian Washing His Hair.*

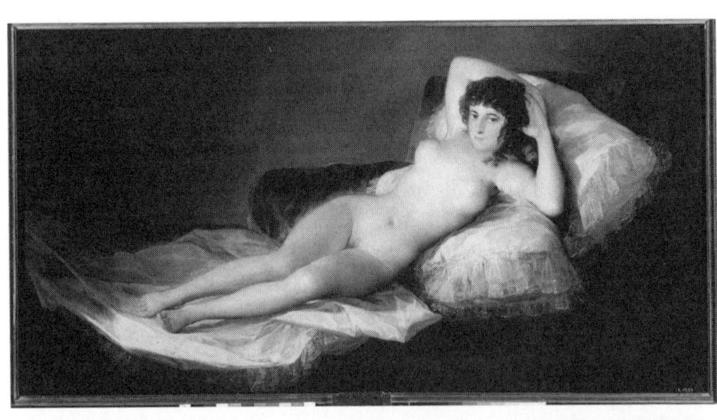

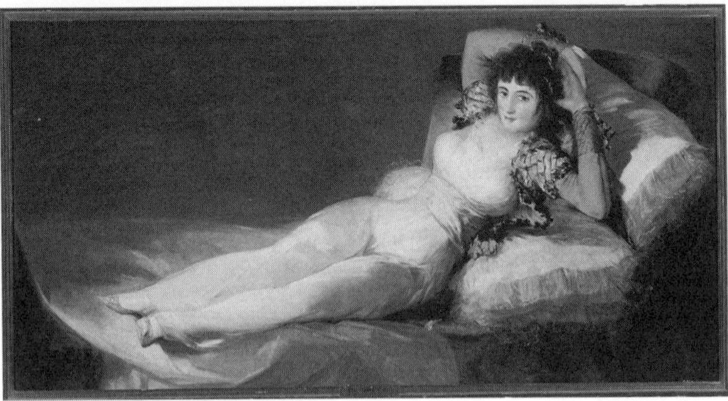

Goya

In an old lexicon from Madrid, *maja* refers to a stylish girl, proud and seductive. The masculine *majo* refers to a stylish man, courageous and confident. The term's etymology is debated, but it seems in the end to be linked with the erotic.

Shedding its native language and sense, slipping toward a proper name, *Maja* became the title and subject of one of the most famous nudes in the history of painting. It may even be the most famous between the *Venus of Urbino* and *Olympia*. It (or she) was certainly not painted without reference to the former of these (and to some other forerunners, such as Velasquez's *Venus at the Mirror* and Titian's *Danae*, both of which were part of the private collection to which Maja would belong), just as *Olympia* was certainly not painted without reference to the Venus of Urbino and the *Maja*. The three are, before all contemporary transformations, like three stations or three figures in an exposition of the female body. But while the two others can be related to other nudes that their painters painted, the *Maja* is an exception in Goya's work. The nude for him, this nude, is not a theme but rather a limit to pictorial thought. However, at the limit, a thought is always confused and anxious.

Moreover, the *Maja* is distinguished by two particular features that should be considered together. On the one hand, shortly after the *Nude Maja*, Goya painted a *Clothed Maja* almost identical except for the clothing. The latter is said to have been hung in front of the former to conceal it. That did not stop the Inquisition from having both of them seized. But the need for concealment did not require that the painting that was to be the screen feature the same model, this time clothed. After all, dressing is not reducible to hiding and always promises or reminds one of a possible undressing. Yet the one who is undressed here is completely undressed; unlike the nudes of Titian and Manet, she does not cover her pubic area with her hand. Her pubic hairs are discrete but conspicuous, if not ostentatious. They are even more so once we think of the time period: Aren't these pubic hairs the first in painting, or not far from it? This motif makes the demand for concealment stronger, but it is not very helpful in explaining why one would put an article of clothing on the naked body in order to conceal it— clothing that is itself diaphanous, intimate, ready to be removed, and whose fabric covers the light curls at the bottom of the belly but all but doubles them in the process. Clothing and nudity motion to one another as though destined for or offered to one another.

Together, these two features lead us to believe that the double *Maja* is neither just a nude flanked by its clothed double nor just two versions of the same portrait. This is because there is no determinate portrait (no one believes that this is the Duchess of Alba anymore), and in any case it is not about that. It is about a *mis à nu,* "making naked," just as one says *mis à mort,* "putting to death." It is a making naked that undresses without remainder and without modesty. The clothed one informs us that the naked one was undressed or undressed herself, that she shed what was left of her reserve.

What does this immodesty mean? What does it mean, this offering of a body whose voluptuousness—so obvious and well formed—is unique in Goya's work?

The other naked or half-naked women in Goya's work—who appear rarely and are small in scale[10]—are sorceresses or old women. In one painting, a woman is undressed, then stabbed by a bandit; in another, a naked woman's throat is slit by two men, who are also naked.[11]

Is the voluptuousness of the *Maja* as assured as we at first think it is, or as we want it to be?

Let's take a closer look. As has often been remarked, the woman's pose is not very convincing. Her arms do not look as though they could remain raised for long, and rather than supporting a reposing head, they have the job of raising the bust and breasts, which look as though they're still being held up by the corset that has been removed. The armpit that is revealed completes the monstration (or demonstration?) of a body that is very intentionally turned toward us. Finally, the gaze says: look, I am offered, I show the image and the idea of a woman who is offered . . . but am I? Or, to whom am I offered? To whom am I offered in painting? To nothing other than to painting and to the pose.

A wave of irony washes over this body that I suddenly see is too willingly disposed to be in a state of abandon. Maybe there is nothing to touch in this nudity that shows nothing but defiance. Maybe the *vestida* is not the one who undressed herself, but is the one who will conceal the *desnuda*, veiling her skin beneath gauze, tulle, and silk, revealing naked skin as another envelopment, and revealing the *mise à nu* as a *mise en retrait*, making withdrawn. If everything in the two paintings indicates the transparency of light fabric, isn't this to emphasize that transparency ceases with the skin, or that its incarnation does not give access to anything, not even to itself?

Another interpretation emerges of the oeuvre of which this work is a part, albeit subject to an internal exclusion. Another interpretation, or the same one extended and darkened. If the flesh is offered in the irony of an undressing ready to be covered up and dressed again, the woman—or the painting or the painter—knows that she is provoking a desire furious with disappointment and is causing an uproar. Insolent and untouchable, the icon of generous flesh becomes blurred, and its carnation announces a carnivorous cruelty. My desire, exasperated by the ostentation of artifice, has no choice but to be bruised or to bruise.

Another of Goya's paintings depicts a "*maja* with a masked man." Some others depict a "maja with Celestine" (an old woman, like many others in his work). Yet another depicts "two *majas* on the balcony," and another "two *majas*," one of whom reads a letter with a mocking expression on her face: there is always a perverse combination of looks, or *memento mori* mixed with defiance. At bottom, these are *vanities,* and Maja's pubescent flesh is not any happier than it is terrible.

Everything does not end there, however. Once again, the one who is dressed undresses herself, or the nude puts her clothes back on, but the light crumpling of clothing woven for intimacy, made for unveiling and disrobing, wraps the tragedy in a suspense that is undecidable. Maja is not cruel. She takes pleasure in the shock of desire and in knowing that the unbearable is imminent, that the shipwreck will happen (another of Goya's canvases,

other naked bodies). I must understand, in my desire and disappointment, that all nudity drowns itself in its own impossibility,
and in its own painting, where its offering is suspended and forever reserved, drowning us along with it in the depth of the
image that it is.

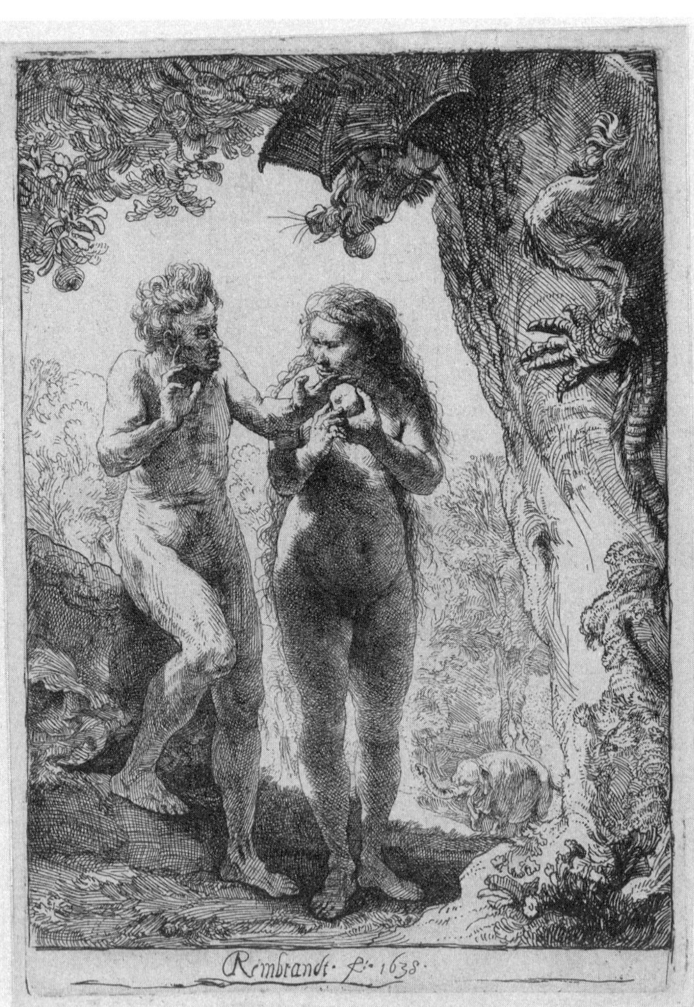
Rembrandt f. 1638.

Humus

The scene is played out in the place and at the moment when nudity achieves its proper revelation. It is the scene where nudity is undressed, or laid bare. The gesture that Rembrandt captures as it is being made, the quick, tense movement that he immobilizes with his strokes is the gesture that will reveal humanity to itself as nudity. Only just emerged from the humus from which his creator drew and shaped him, man (*l'homme*, he who is made of earth, *homo*/*humus*) is about to see himself and see himself naked, that is, exposed to an indetermination that removes him from nature or essence. More precisely, the man and the woman, who are one flesh, are going to see one another naked, the flesh that becomes two by being exposed, naked.

The elephant passing through Eden in the background represents a nature that is not exposed, that cannot be rendered naked, that is enclosed in a carapace: an assurance or affirmation that does not care to affirm itself. In contrast, the woman and man tremble with an affirmation that passes through them and exceeds them as much as it grips them. This is represented by the dragon, a figure whose extravagance could be described as Satanic evil as well as it could suggest its fabulous, invented character. In reality, it must be understood that sin is nothing in itself; it is a twisted, gleaming fantasmagoria laid over nudity.

But sin is nudity: it is not to be clothed in the attributes of a destination, of a congruence with the order of nature and to find oneself, by contrast, given over to the task of creating an origin, of inventing one (in the way the dragon is invented), or even of venturing beyond all origin, that is, into the very crucible of origin: into the nudity where the origin unveils itself as what it is, that is, as not given, not ready, not available, under way, open like the woman's cleft at the center of the scene. Original sin: the failure to be clothed in an essence.

As a result, embarrassment can be seen mingling with trembling, with a waiting that can already taste the risk that it is going to take, the sour taste of the fruit that is forbidden only because it is not yet anything and because it has to be invented, ripe fruit from an origin that has not yet bloomed [pas encore éclose].

These bodies must therefore be on the verge of being exposed and exposed to one another. The woman's body is heavy. It weighs on itself, heavy with the weight of earth and desire. The engraved lines and hatch marks emphasize the heaviness of the mass of dark hair and the dark weight of the belly, in the middle of which is engraved a cleft that is visible, as though all the hair had been removed. The naked body begins by weighing. It flexes and twists a little under its own weight, while the hair that falls below her buttocks is like a shimmer of heat, an exhalation of earth warmed by the sun.

Being undressed does not make a body lighter. Quite the contrary. The elephant is lighter, and he indicates this by lifting up his trunk and moving along at high speed. In contrast, embarrassment is weighty and almost shameful. This does not arise out of a prior condemnation of the flesh; this scene has not been preceded by any sort of repression. It is the other way around.

The flesh can find itself blamed only once there is shame, the sentiment that comes with appearing before oneself, the *humility* of the *humus* or *homus* exposed to itself: shown to the other and to oneself, to the other as to oneself, shown as what shows itself.

This is how the sexes were differentiated, as they had not really been before now. The woman is the weight of the body, the man its twisting. The woman is the gaze that watches the gaze of the other; the man is the alarmed vision of the unknown; and this unknown is first of all the nudity of the woman, nudity as such, which is always the nudity of the other, always altering, always inappropriate and therefore improper, the non-origin that originates itself, that emerges from itself, from nothing, that just emerges.

Their hands meet on the fruit, except for Adam's right hand, which is raised to make a sign whose meaning remains unclear: either a warning or an indication of what will happen next. One way or another, it demands attention. We must take notice of what is happening where the hands touch. The fruit is the place of touch: there the bodies are skin to skin. The skin of the fruit is only the surface of this contact. The fruit isn't even for eating. It is what came into the hand, what offered to place itself in the palm and under the fingers (it is presented twice above the couple, on the branch of the tree to the left and in the mouth of the dragon in the center). Its light weight lets the hand enjoy its roundness, which is punctuated by the eye (this is the name for the depression left in the fruit by the calyx of the flower). This eye is the gaze of nudity on nudity, as is, further down, the navel of this woman who was not born of any mother: origin without origin, the fruit that precedes every flower, the original absence of natural blooming [*éclosion*].

The fruit organizes the touch and trembling of the bodies; it offers itself as a summing up of their rounded volumes; it is a breast and a buttock, a belly, a cheek, and always at the same time the eye that allows us to see how much the body is exposed. For the body is fragile, like the fruit, and in enjoyment it comes undone as the fruit comes undone when it is eaten. It trembles from being close to both its touch and its disappearance, its pleasure and its death, at the same time. This is no longer a couple of mortals facing the immortal gods. This couple tastes its death. It touches the confusion of being between man and earth, *homme* and *humus*, fertile earth and life visited by death, the flower that disappears into the fruit, spirit passed into body, humble and shameful but drawing from the earth a strange, fragile splendor, the emotion of bodies as they face one another, shrinking from revealing themselves.

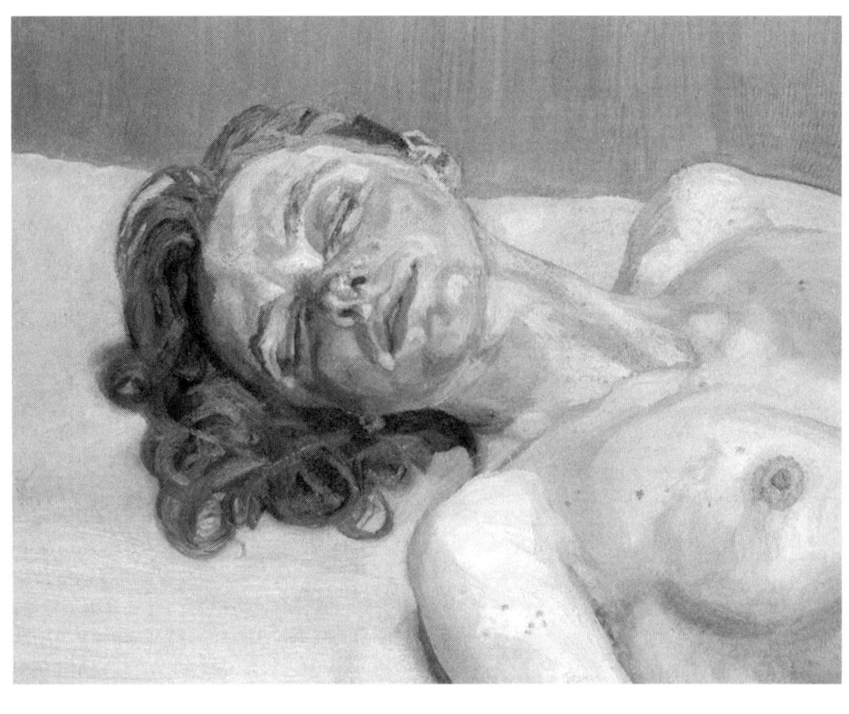

Incarnate

The nude sets us before an a-symbolism that is, as Michel Deguy pointed out in an old essay on Bataille, also an a-theology that strips the divine of all forms of transcendence, an immanentization of the divine body.[12]

In this sense, the pink [*incarnat*] of the nude is exactly the stripping of incarnation: an incarnation without redemption, without spirit, without Word, without epiphany. All that is left is the palpable matter of color that makes flesh: the mute surface of nudity.

Lucian Freud's pictures, and their extraordinary pink, make us *feel* flesh. They don't provide an image of it but show the very consistency of it. There are tangible traces of the meeting of color and canvas, of the hand that draws the lines of the body, and of the flesh that is incarnated in the color. The weight of the Krems white that Freud uses, which has twice as much lead oxide as other whites, doubles the consistency of the flesh and gives body and life to the nude. But it also allows the penetration of the flesh—precisely, *in-carnate*—and enters into the intimacy of the nude.

Intimacy, which is innermost and most deeply hidden, becomes the surface. The interiority of this nude is the surface incarnate. The nude is spread across the surface of the painting. The eyes are closed, the muscles relaxed. This is abandon, complete exposition to others. Without this complicity, without this trust in the other, without this unreserved letting go, the nude could never be incarnated in its reality.

The incarnate is the subject that withdraws; those are its eyes that close, making it so that only skin is exposed, defenseless, to the gaze and the touch of the other. The incarnate is the threshold of *eros*.

She's asleep. I look at her in silence. My eyes lightly touch the consistency of her body, its intimacy, its strangeness. I love her. I love it.

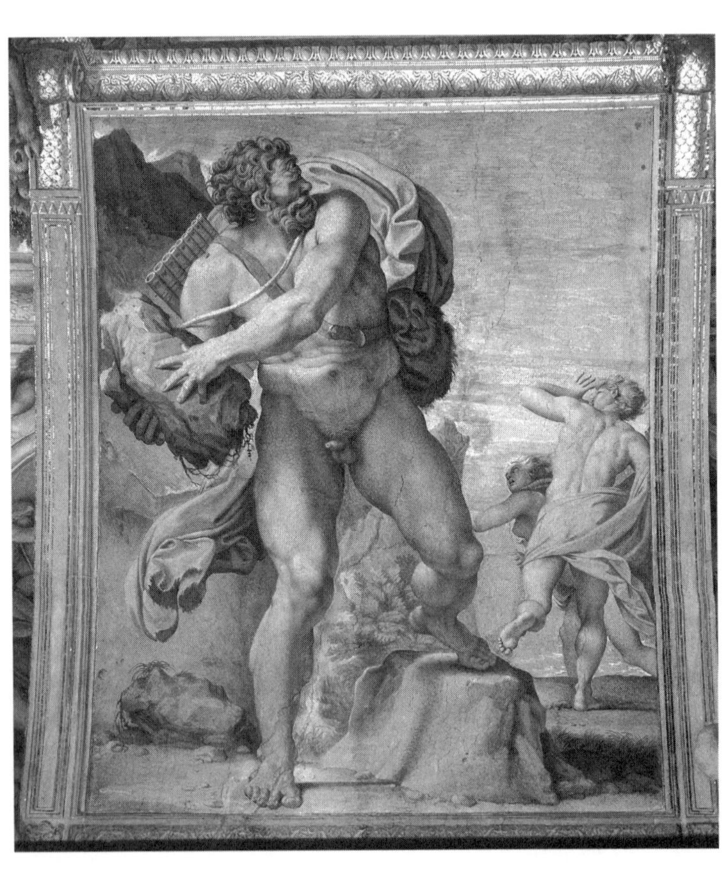

Joker

Of all human nudity—and there's no other kind of nudity—the penis is the only part that reveals more than, or something other than, nudity. It isn't skin, or it is no longer only skin, but is as uncovered as skin. There's nothing to push aside, neither hair nor lips, in order to expose the penis that the patch of hair presents and doesn't hide. It's there to be seen, not suspended between the thighs, as is it is often said to be, but in front, flanked by its family jewels. Nudity here lacks any reserve of modesty. The skin is not the luminous transparence of the body: it is only an organ and an additional limb. In truth, the body is left behind: we are before another presence that is singular, independent—and hanging out. Either the penis falls, almost shapeless and crumpled, an awkward pendulum, or it's erect, swollen, huge, powerfully in action, with meaning and presence only in ejaculation.

The *mimesis* of the body is struggling here, even broken. One can only paint a penis by nesting it in the hollow of thighs that are close together, like a little ball caught in the fleece of pubic hair. That's the way it is often depicted in classical painting when vine leaves or shells are not used. One might say this shows the great beauty [*vénusté*] of the penis (and therefore its feminization). But the erect penis can't be painted (or photographed) without being pornographic, that is to say, without revealing a *methexis* without *mimesis*, a contact, a contagion that dissolves the representation. The penis is the joker of the naked—but an uncompromising joker, forever too improper really to be put into play.[13]

Yet Carracci succeeds in treating the untreatable. Polyphemus the Cyclops has just caught Galatea, the object of his romantic desire, in the arms of Acis. He raises the rock that he is going to throw at the young man. Polyphemus's penis is thrust forward by the movement of his entire body (just as the piece of loose fabric to the right reveals his penis in its nudity). Although it's raised, the penis isn't erect: in this instant, it is held in the middle between its two possibilities. However, its tip is open: a lighter circle there makes this clear. Corresponding with his shining orifice are the nine mouthpieces of Pan's flute that the giant carries on his back. Ovid's text specifies that it is "an enormous flute, composed of a hundred reeds."[14] One hundred could be represented by ten, the tenth reed therefore being the penis. It isn't going to ejaculate; it's going to sing or whistle while Polyphemus shouts (*polyphemus* literally means "one who has many voices"). This musical sexual organ is raised like a little trumpet that has just escaped the embarrassment of being a misshapen trunk or a rubicund cudgel. Polyphemus has a harmonious boner, and for once the penis can exhibit itself right in the middle of a painting. However, this harmony is ironic: changed into a sonorous pipe, the penis misses out on the sexual pleasure it was after.

The irony is made even stronger by the presence of the volcano on the slopes of which the scene takes place (Etna, as Ovid specifies). To the right of the giant's head, we can make out a spurt of fire on the mountain, while to the left of his thigh, at the same height as his penis, a second crater holds open its fuming mouth. Sonorous or gaseous, this penis only spurts air.

There is more. Open, in the center of the scene, the phallic mouthpiece is eye-catching, but perhaps it also plays the role of an eye turned toward the spectator, as so often appears in painting. The Cyclops's one eye looks up at the sky; Galatea's eye, looking back, rolls upward; and Acis protects his eyes. But the penis offers to us a blind and obscene orbit, a sort of comic menace. It is as if to the spurt from the rocks beneath which the crushed Acis's blood will gush out to form a river, there corresponded a spurt of paint in our eye, which is nothing but Polyphemus's furious spasm and the painting of desire, which cannot be represented.

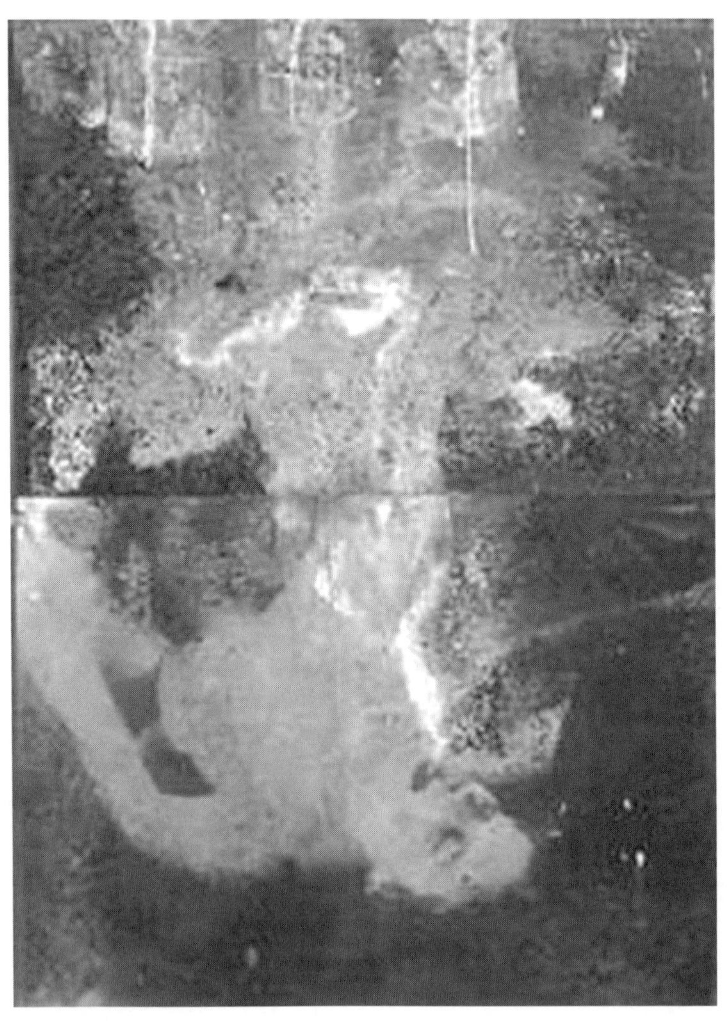

Khaos

In the beginning, there is Chaos: the first of all the gods to be born from nothingness, and the only one to remain after they have all disappeared. After it, Gaia, with her vast bosom, appeared, and so did Eros. Chaos, Gaia, and Eros are the knot from which the history of the world and the mortals who inhabit it develop.

Because it is the original state of the disorder of matter, Chaos is at the beginning, a beginning that precedes all beginning without, however, being anterior to it. It is a beginning that is simultaneous and always pending. It is a beginning, therefore, that is not only an origin but also below and beyond all origins, a caesura, an initial deflagration that accompanies all the steps of humanity. This departure spins off in no particular direction. In it, up and down change place and lose their meaning. Chaos is the confusion that exists before creation—pure matter, ablaze.

It is a gaping, bottomless opening, over which float the figures that fix it in place. They fix it in two senses of the term: they make an image of it, immobile but broken, and they peer into the pure possibility that it is—always in motion in its indetermination.

Chaos hangs over and subtends the human, and the erotic nudity of man. The nude inhabited by Eros appears or surges up from the chaos of matter. Between the naked body's undulating and vibrating lines, a figure takes shape, in an extension with uncertain contours, like a pure plastic or material signification.

In fact, the nude is still matter, but matter that is produced after the division of sense. (The painting is bi-partite: it is the bi-partition and the oneness of sense). It is no longer first matter but figurative matter, pictorial matter, rhythmic matter. If chaos is noise, the nude is rhythm; if the former is a mark, a plane, the latter is line, figure.

But the nude does not elude or suppress chaos. First matter continues to come from it or reenter it. In a certain way, the matter of the nude conserves in itself traces of the deflagration from which the partition of sense has issued. From one opening to another, matter continues to flow out, from the original opening to a wide-open mouth. ("Chaos, *khaos*, *khaino* means 'to yawn'; it signifies something that opens wide or gapes," Heidegger writes.[15]) The nude: not a "beautiful form," but chaos in the order of the body, an opening in the closing of the figure, anarchic matter in the middle of the laws of composition.

The naked figure eroticizes Chaos and creates a point of contact: in the nude, one touches the partition of sense, at the edge of the composition. "Plastic conviction" (Roberto Longhi[16]) gives birth to the figure drowned in the Chaos of first matter. Pictorial matter touches living matter and gets back into touch with a reality that, from now on, is neither in the painting nor outside of it. It is on the edge, in the partition of the senses.

The nude: not only aesthetic—and this goes for art in general—but also an eroticism of matter and form. To touch matter's eroticism is to sense the sense of the nude.

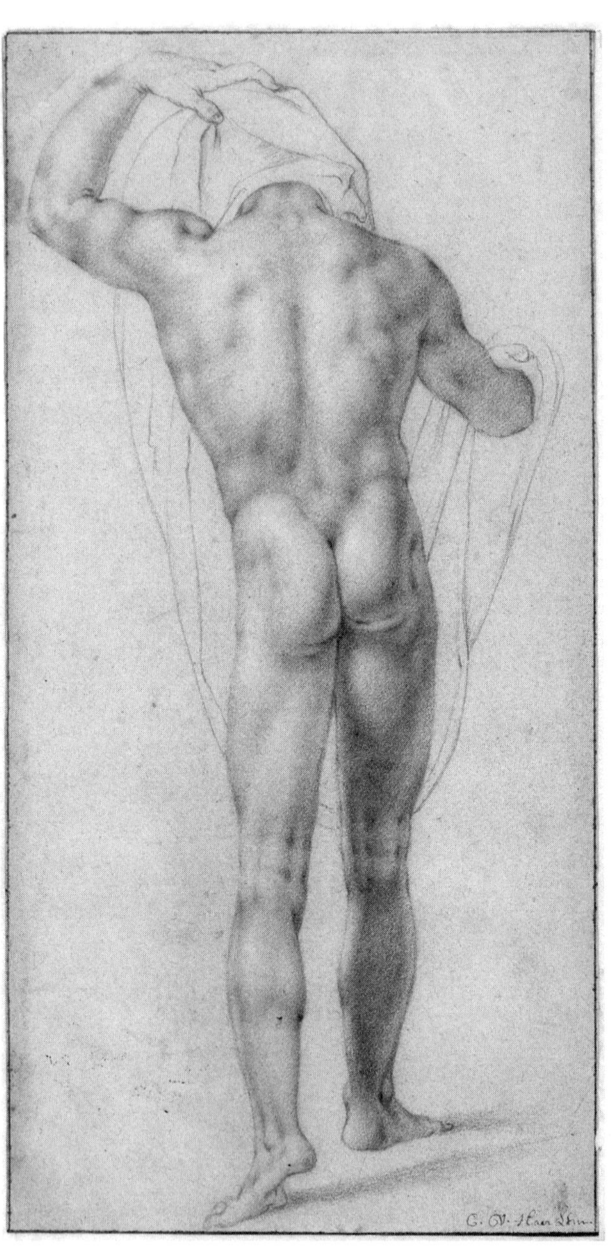

Lumbar

We are faced with a back. A back, rather than a face, is facing us. It's not that someone has turned his or her back, since he or she hasn't turned around. He hasn't turned away from us, and we also don't anticipate him turning toward us. He approaches us with his back. He presents himself from the back, and it is as a back that he is present. Nudity here is the nudity of the back.

This naked man (if it is a man) is undressing, and he holds the cloth that he has almost finished taking off, the shirt that he lifts and stretches above him, as though it were also supposed to shroud his head in order to better reveal his back. It's a large, old-fashioned shirt, maybe a nightshirt, and it falls in front of his body down to his knees. This is how we know that the entire front of the body is hidden from a spectator that we could imagine standing symmetrically opposite us, in the background of the drawing or, through a secret tear, on the other side of the paper. In fact, the cloth of the shirt meets the texture of the paper, and they blend together in thin marks that are absorbed into the background. Ultimately, this body has no front, not even a possible or virtual one. It is entirely within its back, totally a back in front. More than this, its front has become its back.

The back holds and exposes the force that holds the body up and carries it forward. It isn't the face; it is the push that allows a body to face up to things. It is all about this push and power: it is a framework of muscle and bone. Everything in it is vigorous. It has nothing to do with the stomach that digests, nor with the face that senses, nor with the sex organ that keeps watch. From the shoulders to the heels, no part has a relation with anything other than the comportment, posture, and machinery of the body.

Because it is facing us, this naked back is not leaning back: its nudity consists precisely in the fact that it does not refer to any foundation or support behind it. It has nothing behind it, and one could say that it has no behind. It turns the back into the front, but puts it in front in a movement that carries it ahead of itself, ahead of us, indeed taking us around the back with it in order to hold us upright—not leaning back—committed to standing facing it and facing toward it.

It is a question of its advance and élan, its support, tension, and comportment—but not of its vision, speech, activity, or passivity. It is a posture, not a nature. It is naked right through to the structure.

Cornelisz van Haarlem's drawing shows the joints and tissues, muscles, tendons, and ligaments of this body. Anatomy rises to the surface. It is the body made up of loins and kidneys, the lumbar muscles in separate arches on the back holding the torso on its base and surrounding the junction where the body rises, straightens up, and becomes a featherless biped.

The raised buttocks are tightened on the sacrum, this extremity of the spinal column that was once consecrated to the gods. These buttocks, side by side, close and cover up the loathsome orifice of excrement, which is rarely covered in the animal kingdom. Simultaneously, they are offered to the grip of the desire for that secret, for that tightening, offered to anal pleasure, regardless of the sex of the figure: because there is nothing that absolutely excludes the possibility that this body may be that of an athletic woman. Or rather, whatever it is that plays around the butt and at the center of the back plays with an indecision that is the indecision of sex itself, that traverses and works on the sexual as its proper difference and opening.

(A slit or a hole at the center of all nudity. An opening that does not open onto anything, but that opens nudity as such.)

The naked back is thus, in all its power, the place of trembling and expectation, a place where unmasking and identification are always to come, sunk in the obscurity of the other side of the sheet on which the red chalk lays its warm plasticity.

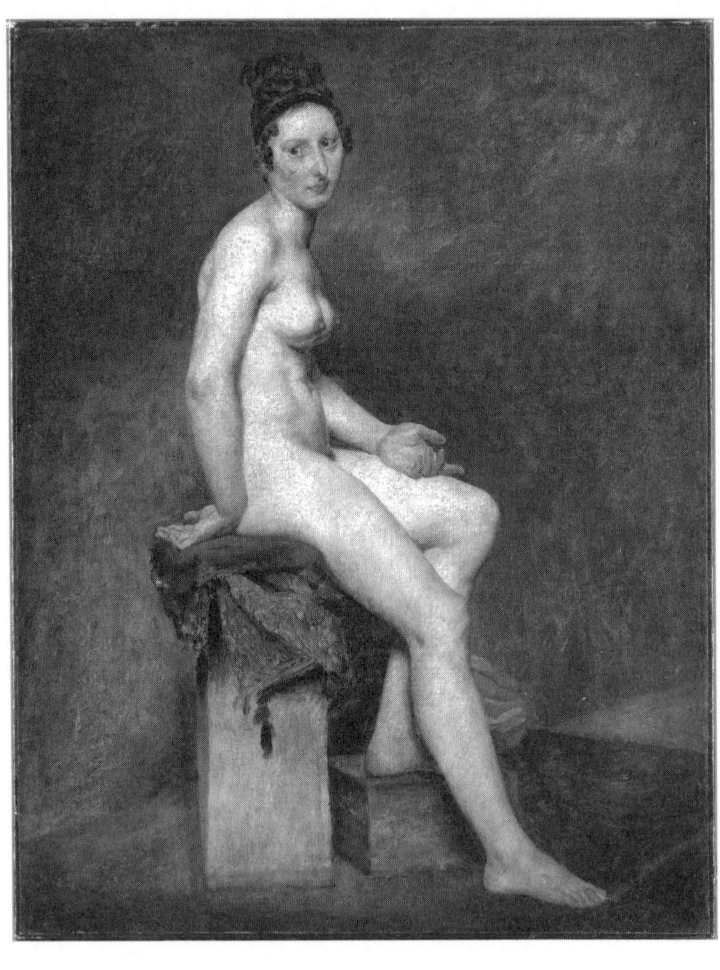

Model

The naked model stands before the painter. To a great extent, the history of painting suggests that model and nude are equivalent: it is the naked body that must be observed, scrutinized, deciphered for its own sake. The clothes, jewelry, and props can be presented to the gaze of the painter in some other way. Painters often make sketches of nude models and then dress the bodies later, on the canvas. But of what or of whom is the nude a model? It is not the model of a general structure of the body, something that the painter knows and that he can reproduce as needed with the help of mannequins or diagrams. The nude is the model not of the body's physical organization but of the intensity of stripping [it] bare. What's presented is not a form to be copied but a force to be received, to bear and to run up against. In this sense, what the model models is not the body but rather the tension with itself that nudity brings about in the body. Naked, the body loses and seeks itself, grasps and abandons itself. It *makes body* with this élan, this restlessness, and this weight of itself against itself.

Here the model is presented as such. The title of the painting is *Seated Nude*, but it is also called *Mademoiselle Rose, modèle de l'atelier de Guérin*. Pierre-Narcisse Guérin was the first of Delacroix's masters, and Delacroix would frequent his studio, along with Géricault, Cogniet, and many others. The same model is mentioned in connection with several other studies by Delacroix and with at least one other painting by the painter Champmartin. In a letter, Delacroix mentions "the buttocks of Mademoiselle Rose" as a sort of metonymy for the work of anatomical study. In fact, everything about this painting indicates that it is a study. The pose is arranged so that the right leg is stretched out and the left one is bent with the left foot resting on a box. The other box or wooden structure serves as a support rather than a seat, the fabric is hastily put in place, the two hands are evidently doing what they have been told to do, the face is turned and tilted to reveal its features while making the gaze absent, the breasts are quite bare and clearly shown, and the pubic area is limited to an allusive touch. Then all this is set against an indistinct background, whose daubing, with the assistance of some highlighting of the outline, only serves to set free the body exposed in its nudity.

This is nothing less than the subject of the painting, which goes well beyond an anatomical study and an exercise in representation. The study or exercise is lost or surpassed in the practice itself. A nude cannot be simply an undressed body, because the undressing cannot be simple. Even when it's completely professional—and in this case we have no reason to doubt that it was, since we have much evidence of the quality of Mademoiselle Rose as a model—it is not the undressing as such that is the object of the painting, nor the *mise-à-nu* or making naked, but the *mise-en-vue*, or making seen. That is to say, it is the *prise-en-vue*, or taking into view, the gaze that grabs hold of the model. It observes her, surely, and copies her. But it sees more than it observes, and it paints something other than what is required for a reproduction. You can search for other copies of Mademoiselle Rose, such as the one by Champmartin (without a doubt painted during the same sitting), or the ones that you can identify among the studies and canvases by Guerin and the other students, but you would not find the same gaze or the same thought in a body that is nonetheless so similar. Delacroix is not far from painting a scene, in fact, the scene of the model. But the model is a woman who knows what she is sharing with the painter and what there is for him to see and imagine: the light marbling that animates her skin here and there and colors her cheeks, the fact that she forgets herself as she submits to the demands of the pose, and this forgetting is a more intense affirmation of presence and reverie.

What is the model (not Mademoiselle Rose, about whom we will never know anything) daydreaming about? She's daydreaming about being a model, about the body as destined to present more than a body, the very idea of a body ("and smooth," as Mallarmé said), and of the proximity and even intimacy of presence. A body is there in the most imposing sense of the word. It is a size, height, and tenderness that must be measured. It is a body exposed in its material specificity and purpose: to embrace and to be embraced, to caress and to be caressed, to become ever more the form of a moved soul.

The model knows all this. She knows that she only shows how she is made in order to show the infinite ends for which she is made. Nudity is a broadening and largesse, an introduction and welcome, glory and modesty, monument and event, all of these together. Here comes a body, a world, a skin whose shadows, with delicate and intense contours, have already gripped us in an embrace: that of the painting with its own body.

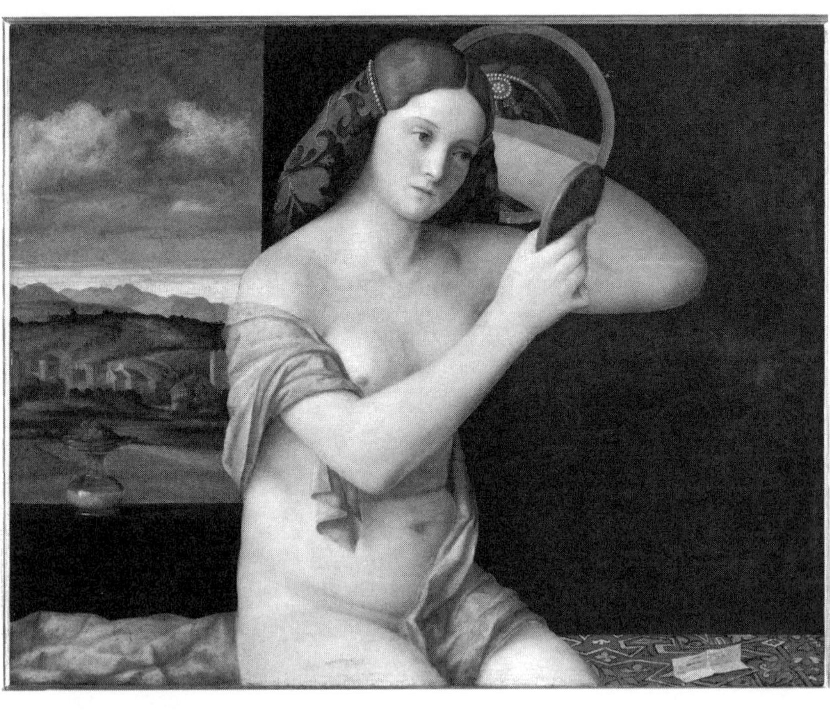

Nimbus

The painting lets us know that it has something to show us in the reflection in the mirror the woman is holding, as another mirror on the wall behind her indicates and emphasizes a law of reflection. On the one hand, the reflection of the arm, suddenly doubling it, accentuating its arch and movement, draws attention to the action of duplication. On the other hand, the reflection of the head highlights the capturing of the back or reverse side, to which the left hand is giving a finishing touch. The two mirrors undoubtedly answer and refer to one another. Their respective frames almost meet, as if they were hinged together, circle against circle. (Might it evoke the haloes of certain Madonnas by the same painter?)

What, then, does the woman see in the mirror? Herself, certainly, just like anyone who holds a mirror in front of her face. But what of herself? That is not so simple. On the one hand, the nature of the scene—someone doing her hair—and the presence of the two mirrors indicate the banal use of reflection, reflection during hairdressing. But on the other hand, the orientation of the little mirror and the presence of the large open window (incidentally, a common theme in many portraits) leads us to assume that in this mirror there is also a partial reflection of the view of the outside.

Since the mirror is tilted up, the reflection can only be of a piece of the cloudy sky. When the woman looks into the mirror, she sees a corner of the sky, and the place where her left hand (the sinister one—let's remember that) arranges or pins the fabric into her hairdo. The fabric is deep blue and full of broad swirls, like the sky. The border of pearls, for its part, answers to the bright yellow band of the setting sun between the sky and the mountains, which appear blue in the distance. The gold of the hair sinks under the wide cloth, just as the brown earth, and its roads and houses, trail off into the distance, toward the mountain and the sky that is heavy with an impending storm.

The woman sees the darkened sky at her back, her back itself, and the back of her head. She sees the background against which her own naked flesh stands out, delicate and superb in its youth, tender, and offered to our eyes as if to a hand that would come to grab this belly and this breast just as it would take the fruit sitting on the windowsill.

The woman sees her nudity from behind: she sees the threat that is at her back, the threat of the storm. She sees the threat because it is within her, reflected in her like the image in the mirror, attached to her like the blue and bronze fabric that swallows her hair, in contrast to the rose-orange veil that reveals her body, plunging at the bottom of her belly, between her thighs, just barely covering her other hair. Her skin the color of dawn matches the crepuscular clouds: the night that comes in the clouds.

To nudity, exposed as the subject of a painting whose geometrical center is found just above the breasts, is apposed—not opposed—its own truth, in the background, like a disquieting depth.

This disquieting strangeness can be seen in the young woman's eyes. She is not actually paying much attention to her hair but is dreaming, troubled, and melancholic. Her eyes reflect—as they say—a gravity without joy that belies the apparent happiness of her body. In fact, this gaze plunges into its own reflection and plunges our own gaze into the return of the self to the self against a background of night and imminent torment, against a ground of ground without ground. Nudity has its death at its back, just as this nude has the cloud behind her. Suddenly we understand that this body, whose gesture traverses the space at a sharp angle, as she folds her arm back behind her, can only last as long as the flash of lightning that the jutting out of her elbow represents, in a reflection that highlights the movement and its brevity. The naked offering is also offered to disappearance.

To the right, on the sill where the woman is seated, a folded note bears the signature "Johannes bellinus faciebat M.D.X.V." *Faciebat* and not *fecit*. "He was doing, he was combing . . ." It is as if his gesture had been interrupted and never completed, like the gesture of the woman, which remains suspended for eternity. It is his own death that Bellini painted, at nearly ninety years old, in this, the only non–allegorical nude that he ever painted (and he painted very few nudes: the *Allegory of Prudence* and *Orpheus*, which is from the same year as this nude and features a woman with a similar look).

It is the death of the painter that is in the background of the painting, like the crow that hovers behind the *Madonna of the Meadow*, and like the sky full of similar clouds in the background of so many others.

The death of the painter is also the death of the young woman. It is the cloud menacing nudity while giving it all of its value, a presence that is both definitive and fugitive. All nudity presents itself before its own death.

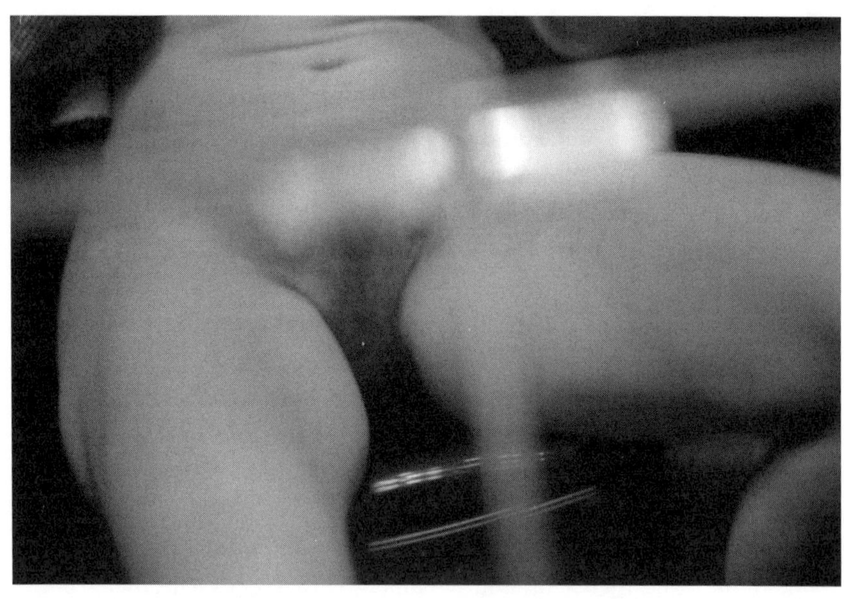

Optic

She enters a place where someone, who knows who, has set up a large mirror in front of which she cannot avoid presenting herself when she has to undress, and undressing is what you have to do in this place. She is exposed to her reflection, which is very close. She goes out again to get her camera. She gets completely undressed, more than the function of this place requires. She sits down and leans back to gain the distance that this narrow space otherwise lacks. She *takes* herself, as they say, offered to her own desire to see herself, to show herself. The lights nearby and the join in the mirror make up a sort of viewfinder that frames her vagina like a target. A beam of light falls along the dark hair, whose shape is lost in the void over which it hangs (disappearance, elimination). It is not Courbet's *Origin of the World*. It is not a womb for conception and birth between open lips. It is a vagina that loses itself in the gaze that it blinds and that is blinded by the reflected light. It is another origin of the world: *fiat lux*. The flash of light that bursts out is *lux*, not to be confused with *lumen*, the light that falls on things. The sun, death, and sex: we cannot look straight at them because they do not have a face. They are each an access to the absolute, the infinite, real impossibility, and the intimate obscurity of the image. There is no entry. Access is forbidden, but in an interdiction that gives access—time to be dazzled and to remain forbidden. It's obscene, which in Latin means "a bad omen" or "harmful," "on the wrong side of the sacred." You want to get there and to turn away in the same instant, in the same space. The nude always contains this contradiction and contraction, more or less exposed. It is not a transgression: that stays in place. Modesty retains what obscenity releases, and there is never the one without the other. The nude must be seen, and seeing must be laid bare: when the two meet, there is a black and white chiasm, the optics of the mirror engraved on the optics of the film, a stream of photons against their graphs. Every bulging lens conceals its obscene smudge, and all nudity is a source of light.

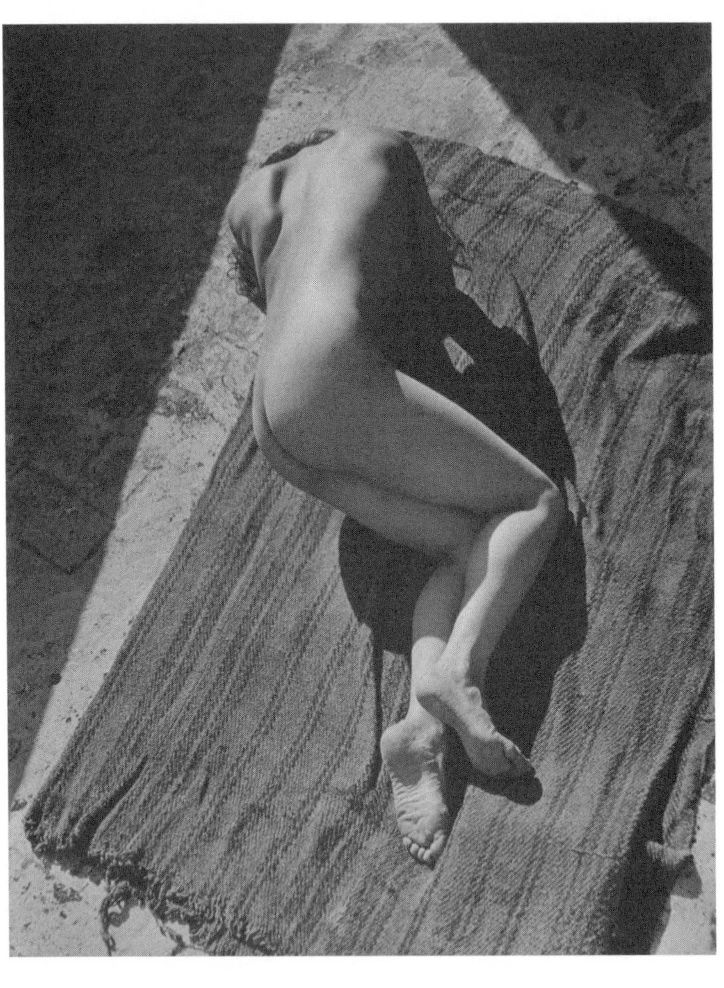

Presence

The nude is *presence* above all, a presence exposed to the gaze of others. A nude, any nude, always finds itself being looked at, even when I am the only one looking. The gaze, when it encounters the nudity of the body, attests to its presence. The naked body is present in the gaze. And its presence is indubitable: it is there.

But the presence of a body is also always *fleeing* the gaze that makes an image of it. When the body is made into an image, it leaves itself, exceeds itself. A body is never given as definitively present to itself or to others, even though it is also not pure absence. The vision of the naked body is exactly the experience of this presence that always flees into absence, into the impossibility of being an immobile given. My body is never given. All of the nude self-portraits are there to prove it—Francesca Woodman, for example, constantly demonstrates this in her work. In her photography, all of this fleeing presence is embodied. All true photography of the nude shows the way that the indubitable presence of the body is always at the same time the anticipation of a gaze and the projection of the subject outside of itself.

Tina has her back to us. She is in a cone of light, and her position is unstudied. Weston makes a portrait of the intimacy of a beloved body that shows itself without modesty. (Edward Weston and Tina Modotti, in the "Mexican years," between 1923 and 1926, were joined in a profound artistic and love relationship.) The intimacy of this nude—the intimacy of the nude—shows in a clear way that what is most intimate is not enfolded in interiority. It is, on the contrary, always completely exposed in the light, to the gaze that comes from the outside. Nudity is exactly this exit from the self that embodies the body. And it is therefore also the experience of a "becoming-subject," but a subject without a face. Paradoxically, the subject looks at its body's shadow, the way in which it leaves itself and leaves the body. It waits for its own beholding of itself, starting with the presence of its naked body. The subject is the anticipation of its indubitable presence. Its presence is therefore also its own suspension, the presence of a nudity of presence, in which what is at stake is not only the subject but nudity itself. It is not an alternation between the positivity of a plain presence and the negativity of a hopeless absence, but rather the everyday oscillation and vibration of something past and something that is not yet, in the luminosity of an imperceptible, ungraspable coming to presence. Almost a specter, but a real and consistent specter.

Every day, in the most common gestures, in the most intimate positions, there is the experience of nudity without grandeur and without model, without the possibility of being captured: the way a shoulder blade juts out, a blanket, a fold in the skin, a shadow, the rhythmic line of a movement. The disappearance of all interiority, exposition of the nude, testimony to a presence. Pure exposition of the intimacy of the self, set outside itself, in the absence of (a) self, and exposed to the other (than) self. Movement of presence from self to self in the nudity of a bare space.

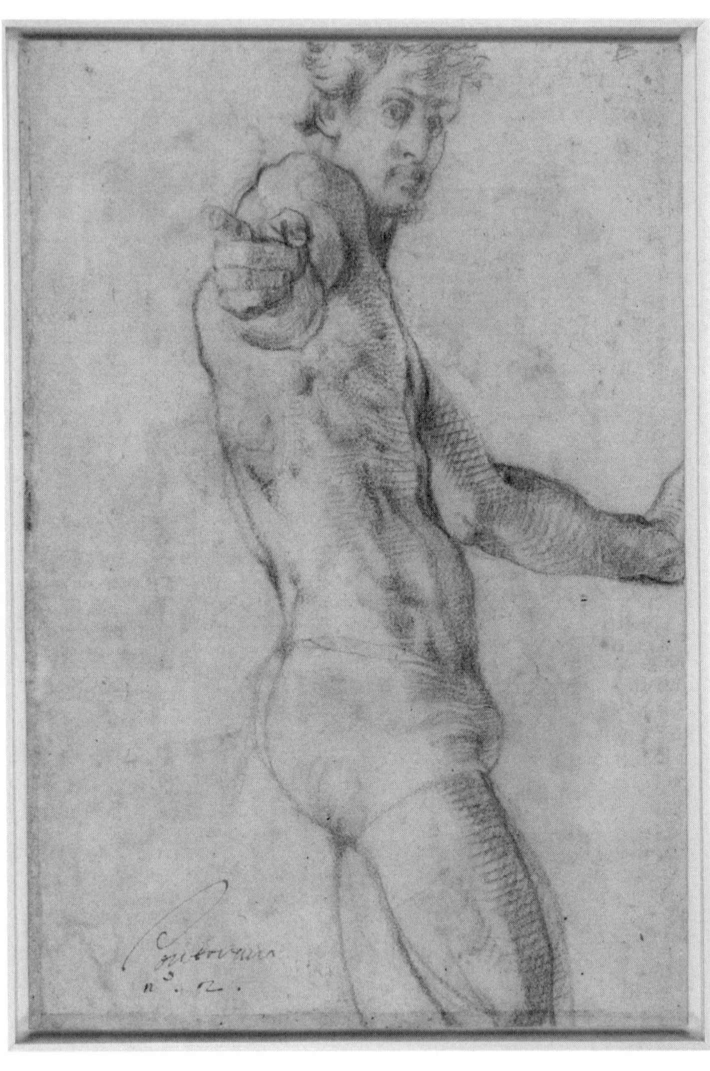

Quodlibet

Among the different possibilities that the figurative arts offer for representing the nude, drawing is perhaps the most surprising, given the lack of means at its disposal. Drawing uncovers the art of the nude, turning the body over to its ephemeral presence.

In Renaissance drawings, on both large and small pieces of paper, bodies multiply; they fragment, they double. Next to a central figure appear hands, feet, legs, torsos, the gluteus, the big toe, noses. Often these drawings are studies done as preparation for works still to be completed; sometimes, the subjects represented don't seem to refer to pictorial compositions at all. Rather, they seem complete just as they are. These are liberated drawings, and drawings liberated from every kind of instrumental use. "Free sketches," as Janet Cox-Rearick calls them, they are drawings that have their own life and therefore are occasionally signed and dated. The sketches, the paper, the drawings, especially when they function as portraits (which was the case starting in the middle of the fifteenth century, both in Northern Europe and around Florence), take on a value well beyond a mere preparatory sketch. "Drawings," as Giovanni Agosti observes, "do not exist only for practical purposes, but need to be seen as testifying to the ability of the artist: thus our interest isn't only iconographic but is also much less instrumental." Many drawings become autonomous "works" before becoming precious gifts, valued pieces of a collection (beginning with Botticelli's *Allegory of Abundance*, moving on to Mantegna's *Judith*, and ending with what Wilde and then Hirst singled out as the presentation drawings of Michelangelo, drawings more or less finished that the artist would give to his closest friends). Sabba of Castiglione, himself a great collector of art, recalls in his *Ricordi* (Bologna, 1546) giving voice to a new sensibility concerning these drawings and sketches: "a sketch, a rough draft done with a simple charcoal and pen that in its characteristics is no less pleasurable than figures of gold . . . such that in the sketch one sees and understands the nobility of art better than in other works made and colored with so much delicacy and effort."

In Pontormo's *Self-portrait in Underpants*, on the right we see two highly realistic preparatory figures for the *Supper at Emmaus*, which probably date to 1525. This was a crucial period both for the painter of the Florentine School and for all of Italian art. Here Pontormo exposes the drawing to the intimacy of art, to its most essential dimension. We might think that in such a bare [*nudo*] self-portrait we can hear echoes of the conversation that Jacopo must have had with Leonardo Buonafé. It is Buonafé who was portrayed at the right of the drawing, then inserted to the left of Christ in *Supper at Emmaus*, a work conceived for the convent of the Certosa of Galluzzo. Buonafé was responsible for the iconography of the monastery of the Certosa, and thus we can hypothesize that in the words quoted above we can also make out Erasmus's antidogmatic teachings and calls for renewal. Indeed, Pontormo's self-portrait seems to have been inspired by a deep antidogmatism. It confronts us with a drawing that is no mere study but shows, almost programmatically, the *pietas* and astonishment of a new gaze opposite a body—opposite one's own nude body. This is not a subject completed for another; what takes form on paper is only that which gives pleasure, *quod libet* ["what pleases"]. In other words, this drawing is the sign of an art and an artist that work for the pleasure of doing and not in pursuit of a craft: an art, as Pontormo will write in his famous letter to Varchi, that wants "to make its works rich and full of various things, working—how can I put this—where splendor takes place: nights with fireworks and other similar sights, air, clouds, lands distant and near, houses that give different perspectives, animals of all kinds and colors, and so many other things." Every subject, in other words, is a "good" subject: *quotlibet ens*, whatever it is, but also whatever it is that is pleasurable and gives pleasure. Thus we have the body, with its realistic masses of muscle standing out in the area traced in red chalk, marking lines of cartilage that merge together in work influenced by the Florentine School just as they do in Northern Europe. There one finds so much of the "unending beauty of every small detail" that Vasari will place the value of the sixteenth century in its descriptively realistic analysis, actually quite close to Dürer. A transition with no solution in continuity with respect to a mental design that gives form to a concept, to an experimental concept, mindful of what is given by accident beyond the canons of dogma. Just as, in the musical *quodlibet* of the sixteenth century, melodies opposed both in form and tone follow and overlay each other, so in the rhythm of Pontormo's elements we hear a continual fusion of styles and an infinite search for a new "varied style" [*maniera*]: Michelangelo and Dürer, Andrea del Sarto and Luca di Leida—the Italian Renaissance and Northern painting.

After having completed the frescoes of Poggio at Caiano and the decoration of Certosa of Galluzzo's great cloister, Pontormo is about to begin the consummate masterpiece that will be the Capponi Chapel of Santa Felicita. His gaze is ready and cannot but turn to itself. The self-portrait is clearly done in a mirror. The index finger is therefore pointed toward his own body, toward introspection and unavoidable responsibility. But the finger, like the gaze, in becoming visible inevitably opens toward the outside while pointing to us, toward someone anonymous and about to appear. Everyone, every body, is called upon by that gaze and that body. A meeting of singular and whatever [*qualunque*] bodies: ours as his. Everyone, in the simple living of his or her life, in the tracing of the plot of his or her existence, in the being of the sketch of a character and a manner of living—all point to the absolute singularity of a style and a stance [*stare*]. An exemplary and unsurpassable drawing, beyond every school and model. The ephemeral trace of a whatever singularity: bodies that overlay each other and touch; that look at and love each other; that are curious about each other—nude and full of modesty, solitary and joined by unmentionable friendships.

—Translated by Timothy Campbell

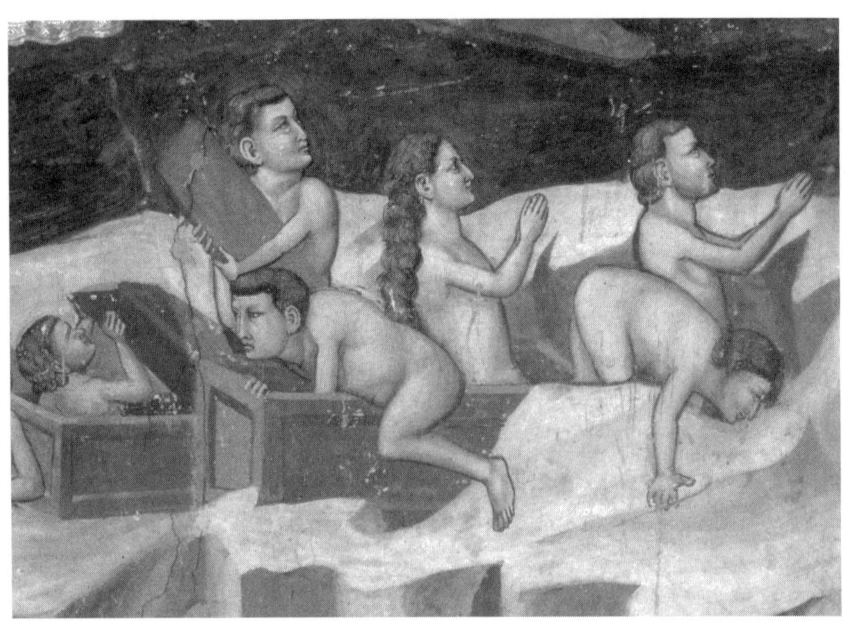

Resurrection

*Kein Gestern, kein Morgen, denn die Zeit is eingestürzt. Und sie
blühen aus ihren Trümmern.* "No yesterday, no tomorrow, because
time has collapsed. And they bloom in its ruins."[17] Nothing but
bodies, naked bodies suspended on a bare wall, in a temporality
that is eternally actualized. It is time completely exposed in the
finite extension of a body. *Paraousia*, the presence of bodies beside
one another. End of the infinite, the infinity of finitude.

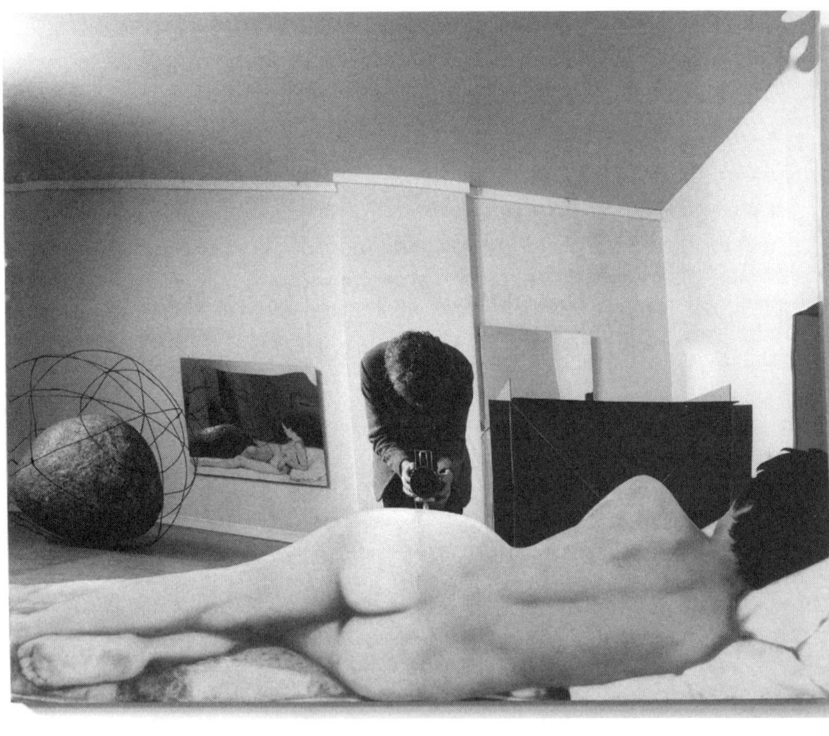

Scopophilia

Before the eighteenth century relatively few nudes were painted from behind, with the notable exception of Velasquez's *Rokeby Venus* (which takes the famous pose of the Greco-Roman *Hermaphrodite*, a sculpture that was initially part of the Borghese collection, was later restored by Bernini, and is now on display at the Louvre). It could be argued that the rarity of nudes depicted from the back in the history of art has to do with a preference for the plastic value of the frontal pose and to the search for a representation of nudity in which the parts of the body exposed to view refer us to the visibility of the face: the one being looked at looks back. The indiscrete gaze of the painter or sculptor is recognized and reflected in the features of a face that rejoices, modestly, in its own corporeality. The frontal nude is in fact almost always marked by the narcissism of the subject represented. Nudity is restrained in part by the purity and neutrality of a conscious and discreet gaze. The delicate but ever-present exhibitionism that accompanies it is thus sublated. In the same way, the voyeurism that guides the work of the artist, and also the beneficiary of the image, seems neutralized. Scopophilia and exhibitionism—the two forms of denial of nudity identified by Otto Rank, among others, in his famous 1911 essay *"Nudity"*—

blend together in the play of complicit gazes between two faces that reflect one another, giving birth to a vision that makes possible a sort of civil inattention, as Erving Goffman might have called it: a fleeting vision that observes without pausing to consider what could cause embarrassment, that passes beyond, that sees without seeing or without making see.

In contrast, in the case of the nude depicted from behind, scopophilia reappears in a powerful way at the moment when the face and the obvious visibility of the gaze eclipse one another. In the return of the repressed, scopophilia in effect passes through the subject's tendency to consider itself invisible to the gaze of others, even though the subject can at any given moment make the desired object visible. The one who sees is not necessarily seen: the reversibility of the visual path must be suspended. The *pleasure of looking*—in all its variations, up to and including voyeurism—is thus expressed in a double drive: both a panoptic will seeking to make visible all that is invisible and the necessity of invisibility. The artist can see but can't be seen; he cannot be recognized in his *philia*, in the voluptuousness of his vision. At the same time, the subject does not see the one who looks at him. And the vision of the one who looks is hampered, even though he wants to see everything. Even the mirror, which could show the hidden side of things, reflects nothing. The nude is given over to its own intangibility, a constitutive invisibility that belongs to it and that is also reflected in the invisibility of the man who is about to take the picture. The volumes of the naked body are hidden from view. The nude thus comes to have a remainder, an invisible but real point that, even if it in principle remains in view, nonetheless slips away. An inclusive disjunction is born. Even in front of a mirror, even if it becomes the very surface of the mirror, the body cannot duplicate its image; it cannot show itself completely. The naked body, entirely at the surface of the mirror, cannot be reflected without remainder. This is the infinite frustration of every panoptic will. Even if we try to duplicate the work and to construct a meta-nude—as Ugo Mulas tried to do when he photographed a work by Pistoletto—the result remains unchanged. The face of the one who sees remains hidden, just like the face of the nude. Its only, authentic face is entirely on the surface. It is no longer possible to go beyond; one can simply be both in and outside the picture, *with* the nude. Beyond, there is only the will of a vision that no longer has a face and that stretches out over the folds of an anonymous and unrepeatable body.

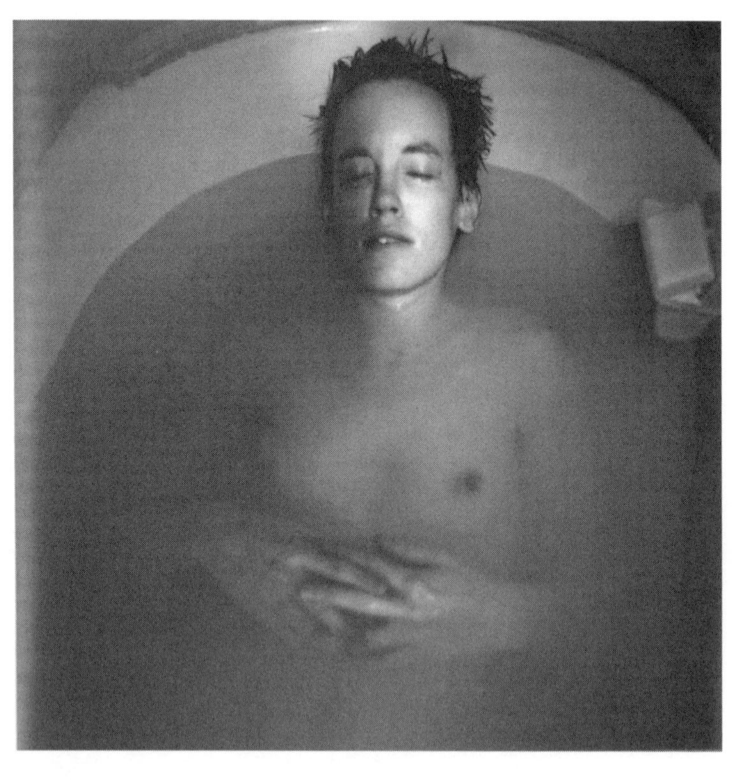

Trans

Jean-Marie Pontevia sees a lack or indeterminacy of sexual identity in Renaissance painting. In his view, there is at the origin of the Renaissance "a sort of hesitation with regard to difference" that makes the categories of feminine and masculine waver, with each continually reappearing in the other across a variety of compositions. On one side would be Leonardo's effeminate men and on the other Michelangelo's virile women. This hesitation, one that is able to make identities vary, would seem to reappear with great power in contemporary art, reaching its limits in the iconography of transgender, whose ostentation is seen as grotesque and banal.

Placing herself in this situation of movement and drift, Nan Goldin offers a different sensibility. Her photographs show us how impossible it is to mark precisely the nude's sexuality. Her subjects are often "trans," but Goldin's originality resides in the capacity to show how the nude, beyond the represented subject, is always this placing into question of sexual identity, this never-ending crossing of identities. In Goldin's best photographs, stretching from the 1976 *Ryan in the Tub* to *Joanna's Back in the Doorway* of 2000, one cannot see what is transpiring; in them movement remains indefinite, suspended. It is here, in the suspension of crossing, that the nude is configured as the infinite transition of sexual identity. But what do we mean by transition?

Mario Perniola defines transition as the passing from a presence to another presence, that is, from something that is to something else that is. (There is no move from a negative to a positive or vice versa, and there is no going beyond.) In the nude it is this movement that is at stake, this crossing of the pictorial or photographic space by the gaze. The gaze does not go beyond but cries out in bare [*nuda*] presence and is not to be referred to the other.

Thanks to nudity, the presence of the other moves space; presence in this case is uncanny, disquieting. More than a simple vision and more than an activating of the sense of sight, the nude is, therefore, a disturbing of the senses, indeed, of all of the senses and in all senses of the word. The disturbance of the soul and of the senses—an arising of sense, in the sense of a body that floats on the surface of the image. Ryan rises up out of the water, immobile and without a gaze. His gaze is negated and opens onto nothing. It is in the eyes of the other, of the one who sees Ryan. The gaze of the nude is blind to itself. It does not know and cannot see itself. It only knows how to be exposed in its absolute trans-parency to the other. The nude appears, moving in the gaze of another body—a bare question of a gaze that vouches for its own existence.

The two gazes—the nude's and that of the one who sees the nude—meet in an indefinite point. Perhaps it is at the skin of the eyelids, this aperture/shutter, much like the diaphragm of a camera, which allows the external world to come inside. And it is in the meeting of gazes, at the limit of the threshold that divides them (and, naturally, at the surface of bodies) that the nude takes on its true significance. The nude is given as a specularity of the gaze and the space that it opens, as a never-ending deferral that hinders fixing one's attention on a single detail. It is as if the impossibility of seeing the point at which two gazes meet forces us to retrace them, to get the eyes moving again, following the curves to see that which always already is placed outside but which is removed from vision: the desire to understand the meeting of that body and that blind gaze, meeting it in our turn. But bodies are not immobile in space. Bodies float and meet and assert their own existence, which is to say, their own being outside of themselves. In this sense, the nude is no longer about absolute immanence, as if the nude enjoyed a defined and apodictic depth, as if nudity, as in *Ryan*, sinks in its own absence of depth. Nor is it about trans-cendence, a moving beyond, a passage to a further dimension with respect to the presumed artificiality of ornament that would cover over the bare [*nuda*] truth of a full presence that is to come. Perhaps it is about a trans-immanence or, more simply (and so as to avoid any misunderstanding), about a passage between two or more presences: that of the trans, which is to say, the crossing that goes so far as to touch, verifying it, the presence of the other, and bounding back to my presence. The meaning of the nude is to be found right at the skin of bodies and in the inexpressible movement from one body to another. Here, then, the meaning of nudity is located completely in the singular experience of a meeting, in the exposition of a body that emerges as if suspended and that opens onto itself and outside of itself toward the infinite. The "trans" of the meeting of nudity and this uninterrupted transition of sense from one body to another is this incomprehensible transference in which the body itself gives itself, in which it experiences itself as its very own outside, as that which comes from outside, but from an outside that is all there. In those breasts, in those hands, in the hair. The transference of the nude is precisely the site of a passage in which the psyche understands itself as

93

extended, as the extension and spatializing that has as a conse-
quence that I have a body, even if that body is never exactly my
body but instead the corporealization of the body in the sharing
of bodies and gazes and their mute "language." The transference
isn't, therefore, a process of identification with the other, nor is
it a projection onto the other, which would presuppose two
already defined subjects. Rather, it is the experience of an exposure to alterity that constitutes the subject. It is exposure to the
stretching that constitutes the psyche. And it is the sharing, at
times painful and at others joyful, of a gaze that emerges from
and ends in nothingness.

—Translated by Timothy Campbell

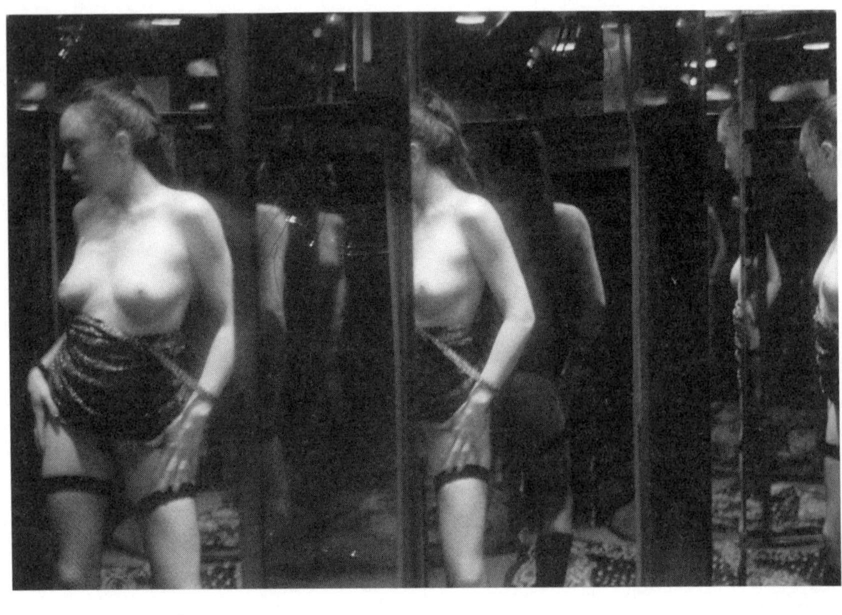

Use

According to its etymology, pornography is a piece of writing, a document, story, or description concerning prostitution. The woman who is prostituted, *porné* (or the prostituted man, *pornos*), is transported to be sold. The verb *pernumi* belonged to the language of exportation, especially the export of slaves. Porn is first of all displacement, transfer: exile, expropriation, deportation. In Latin, prostitution designates a putting forward, monstration, and exhibition. The two lines of exportation and exposition intersect. The nude that pornography lays bare is exported and exposed, stretched and pushed outside of itself, out of its modesty or reserve. Its job is to show that it shows itself or that it's shown, that it's nothing but a being-shown. The spectator gets off not only on what he sees but more properly, or improperly, on seeing and seeing himself see, on seeing the body that he sees is shown.[18] He gets off on seeing and knowing that this nude is shown as such, that is to say, simultaneously as nude and as a nude that's shown. Porn is both vertiginous and abysmal: it shows that it shows itself and shows that, for my part, in making myself show it, I reveal myself to myself as someone who shows what it shows me, one who both shows and is a voyeur.

However, the nude is never only shown; it also shows its monstration. There is no stripped nude that isn't stripping (stripping itself, and being stripped by whoever sees it). In this sense, there's always an imperceptible vacillation between the nude and porn. Not that the difference isn't clear: but it trembles, and this is perhaps also the trembling of modesty. The solution that is often called "eroticism" (or even "seduction," "sensuality," "license") escapes ambivalence and involves showing that one does not show but suggests: it's a hypocritical pornography.

The trembling through which porn and the nude come into contact separates the monstration of monstration from the monstration of the fact that there is nothing that is shown that isn't also infinitely concealed right at the skin. Everything plays out right against the skin: the skin of the nude imposes itself on the gaze, touching and penetrating it, denuding the gaze in its turn, while, in pornography, the skin provokes the eye to function as a mechanical viewer, a prism that disperses the spectrum of getting off. One is the nude of truth, of its infinite coming into presence, and the other is the nude of definite and definitive access to truth, showing all its faces at once. Two sides of exposition, exportation, exasperation.

"Peep Show" signifies "a spectacle for the glance," for a furtive look, keen and secret, an eye that throws itself on its prey, sucking on it and swallowing it like its own globe. It is caught in the trap of representing the unrepresentable. That's why it's poor. It braves this poverty, as the reverse side of nudity, the other face of the spasm, sublime and miserable like the splendor and misery of the courtesans who are constantly troubling literature, painting, and photography, from Mary Magdalene to Olympia, and all the intrigues of painters and their nude models.

Julien Daniel's photo isn't porn but is about porn and the look of a voyeur. The girl is offered behind a pane of glass and reflected by several mirrors. The glass and the mirrors are the prism of an eye that's been reduced to a machine for seeing. The voyeur fantasizes about a scene in which he takes the girl in all ways, from all sides, the body spread, stretched, literally anatomized according to the segments and the shuddering of a coming that shows itself to itself. The fantasy is not an image but always a scene, a scenario that is shown on a loop. What is played is the scene of use: how to use this body, how to use this skin, these breasts, thighs, buttocks, and the slit that the girl presents, exposing a lasciviousness of which she knows she must be the literal text and explicit analysis. "Lascivious" means that which does its utmost to provoke desire. Lasciviousness, a machination of desire, is already on the scene. Between the lascivious and the nude, there is the arc of lightning from engineering to genius. Who can accurately measure this gap?

It exists, however, and it is the difference between use and abandon. The girl shown isn't shown in order to show nudity. She is shown in order to show a beyond-nudity where it's a matter of using and abusing this body no longer looked at but taken, handled, shaken. In a sense, porn speaks truly of sex as shaking, a spurt, some wet grunting. In another sense, which is the same sense turned upside down, it speaks of the impossibility of using this truth. It tries to use and wear out what can't be used or worn out. The truth is just that: one does not use it. The nude is unusable and cannot be utilized. Porn is worn out from the start, worn out in advance as a fantasy of use (which must therefore also be about abuse: exportation, exhibition and the extortion of excitation, putting the trance up for sale, a very vague memory of sacred prostitution). That's why the pleasure of love is devoid of fantasy: it's your body and mine now; this is not a scene. Or rather, the scene always unravels even as it escalates.

The sullen pout of this girl bears all this wear and tear and at the same time participates in the fantasy (a pout closed in on itself, isolating in itself the supposed lasciviousness). Used, tired, and disillusioned after having undoubtedly been abused in order to be put up for sale, she waits for the client to wear himself out. The tendency of the image is to come undone. The scene disassembles; "the posture is dissolved,"[19] as Sade would say. Abuse and usurpation can begin once again to fuck another eye. It is inexhaustible—and it is at the same time as if the inexhaustible aspect of this use, taken up again and again indefinitely (the monstrous accumulation of pornography throughout history, from Aretin to Diderot, to Apollinaire, to all of the "hells" and *curiosa*), continued to tremble close to nudity, which can't be used, exploited, or exposed. Because in this image there is still a nudity that moves us in spite of everything, seized as we are by the sadness that the photo has captured.

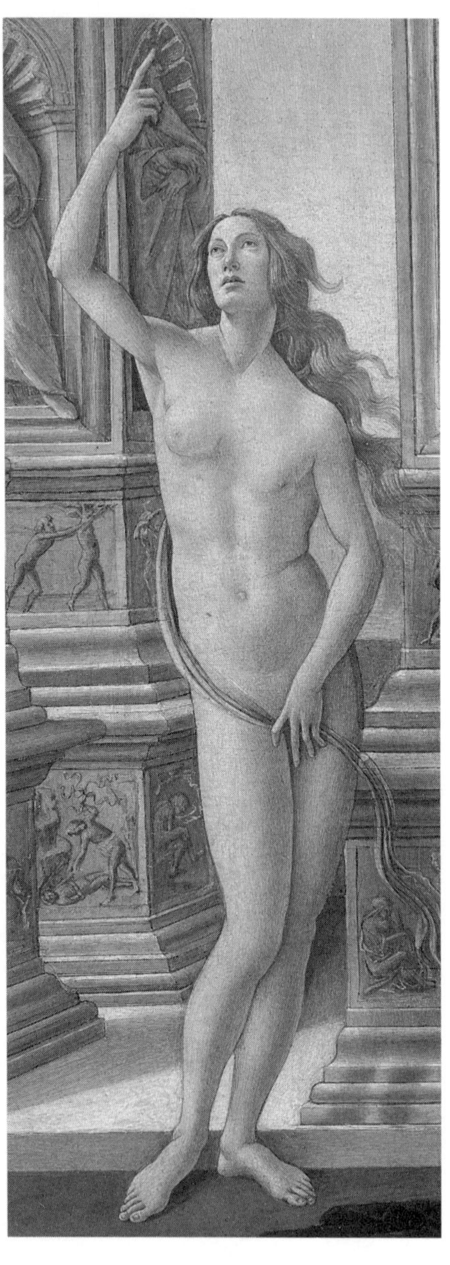

Veritas

Even in the most moralistic times, truth has always been represented as a naked body, and the confrontation with nudity has often been felt to be art's moment of truth, the place where truth is given as art—whether in painting, sculpture, or photography. On this point, Western art is extremely consistent, almost monotonous. The possible examples are innumerable. Take *Truth*, which appears in *Apelles's Calumny* by Botticelli. We find ourselves before the recapitulation of an ideal classical model. One senses still resonating beneath the strokes—even though they are now harder and broken—the sinuousness of Botticelli's Venus. While *The Birth of Venus* was painted under the revolutionary influence of Marsilio Ficino's Neoplatonic theories, encountered in the court of Lorenzo the Magnificent,[20] *Truth* is marked by the return to a severe Christianity, like that preached by Savonarola in the same years in Florence. It is also marked, as Kenneth Clark points out, by Botticelli's probable reading of Alberti's treatise *On Painting*, which defines truth as *pudica et verecunda* ["modest and shamefaced"]. Compared with the curviness of *Venus*, the figure has become drier and more elongated. The finger on the right hand is raised to indicate transcendence. In the same way, the gaze frees itself from the earth. The folds of skin on the forehead form a perfect "V" and draw the eyes of the spectator toward the face. *Truth* is concentrated in the head and in the gaze turned toward the sky. The contours of this figure tell us something different about the body than the contours of Venus do. The gaze is supposed to fall not on the shape of the limbs but on the idea that transcends them, not on the flesh but on the spirit that animates it, not on the body's lines but on the soul's *copula mundi*, which, through the love of beauty, allows one to enter into contact with God, the Good, and the Beautiful. With *Truth*, Botticelli creates an icon of the Greco-Christian doctrine of truth, of the perfect fusion between the Platonic writings and the Christianity of the "Fathers of the Church" (not to mention certain important features of Thomism) that was produced during the Italian Renaissance and in the humanistic ideology that accompanied it. According to such a doctrine—which Botticelli seems to embody—*veritas* is an *adequatio rei et intellectus*, which is to say, conformity between a thing and the idea of this thing. Truth is therefore a relation between a presence, between what is present and what we are constantly encountering, and an idea that imposes itself on the intellect, on this *intellectus humanum* that is always "guaranteed" by the *intellectus divinum*.

Botticelli seems to make truth coincide with the correct vision of the idea inside the soul, according to the doctrine formulated at the end of book 6 of the *Republic*. For Botticelli, the more adequate the gaze falling on the ideal model, the more truth will be given in art; the purer and more naked the gaze—without unnecessary ornamentation—the more art will be true. The nude is the most obvious example of this: truth is the nudity of an idea, not the nudity of the body. The body is a sign of something else, the pure indication of an ideality (the raised index finger indicates the ideal sky). Truth then corresponds not to the nudity of the body that incarnates it but to what transcends it in the invisibility of the *intellectus divinum*. The truth of art is not on the canvas's bare surface but in what hangs over it. The beautiful and the true are *aliquid incorporeum*. The splendor and misery of the classic nude.

But when we look more closely, the underlying question of Botticelli's painting is: What is the idea to which truth's body must measure up? In a way that is a bit peremptory—but in a certain sense very close to Ficino's Platonic interpretation—we could say that the idea is for Botticelli the visible form. It is the intelligible insofar as it takes shape; it is the visibility of the invisible. Ultimately, Botticelli's *Truth* is, precisely, a body. In all of (his) painting, including those images most impregnated with transcendence, there's an attempt to embody the idea, to show the idea as a *visible form*. In art, truth is what configures the idea, what gives it a body, shows its corporeal side; it's the soul's extreme limit, where it becomes visible and extended. The truth of art is the extension of the idea in the coincidence of a soul and a body. In the end, truth is given as the relation between vision and the unveiling of the body, the body of the thing. The Greeks—the very Greeks to whom Botticelli refers—used the word *aletheia* to describe this experience, a term that indicates the place, the opening, in which the thing appears as what it is (Heideggerian *Anwesung*), or, more precisely, where the thing unveils itself, showing itself naked. Greek ontology here resembles Latin ontology in that the latter, in order to define the character of the unveiling of truth, invented the expression *nuda veritas*. The truth of art, the *nuda veritas*, is precisely this articulation in which the soul and the body coincide, where the surface of the body traces the limits of the soul, where the soul is completely exposed to the body's surface. *Nuda veritas*: articulation or disjunctive relation.

Botticelli's *Truth* therefore indicates—certainly in the direction of something that is other than itself—the *nuda veritas* that never coincides with a body and a figure without remainder; but at the same time it does not refer to an object or an essence but to the thing itself, to the naked thing, the nudity of the nude. It is not about the return of an image to a pure transcendence but about the necessity of giving to the gaze a vanishing point from which the thing can present itself in the nakedness of its coming to presence. Truth is this vanishing point. Art is not the putting to work of truth but its being made naked. Neither imitation, nor reproduction, nor copy, but the simple exposition of a naked body: the most general of ideas in the most singular of bodies. The *Anwesung* in which truth becomes visible is certainly the self-presentation of *Anwesen*, of presence, but it is also always an *Abwesen*, an absence. In other words, coming to presence is also a subtraction from presence, an evanescence.

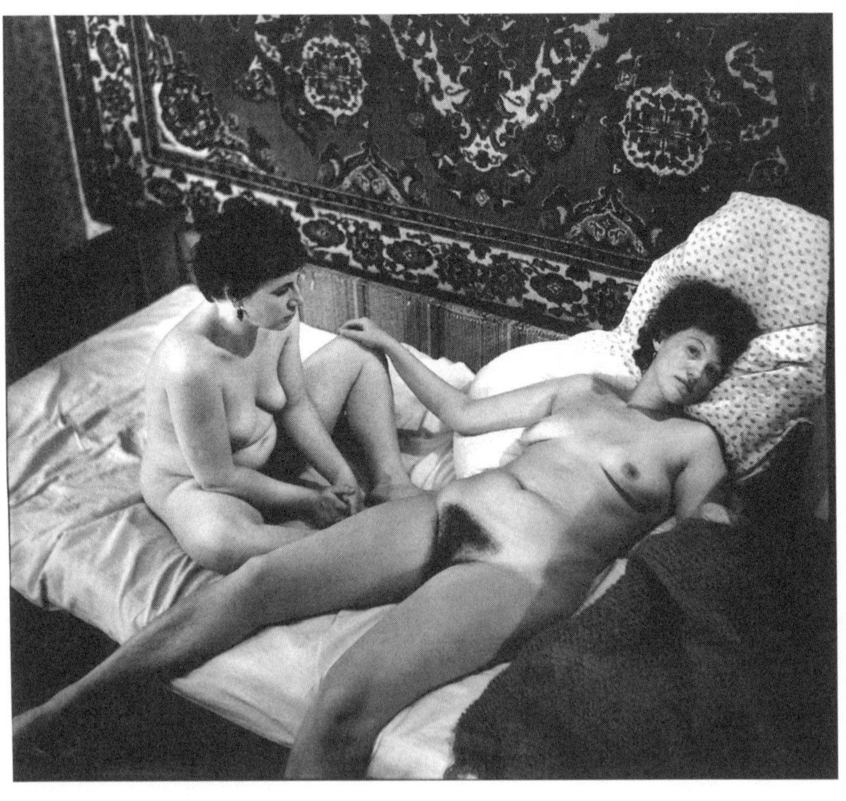

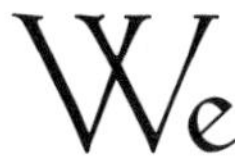

We

We are here[21] . . . we are here; here we are. We are naked and heavy with an undecidable nudity. You can't tell whether we are tired or sated. You can't tell whether we are sad after making love or anxious before it or not daring to do it. Or maybe we have to part, either because separation is being imposed on us or because we have made the decision ourselves. You have no way of knowing, because maybe we don't know ourselves. The photographer arranged us like this. He arranged our tender, ordinary bodies, a great, ordinary tenderness, gently disenchanted. He arranged our gazes: one looks at the other; the other looks blankly into space, toward you but just to one side of you (to one side of the camera). One is cross-legged, watching, waiting, maybe asking. The other is slumped down, spread out on the pillow and the crumpled sheet; she doesn't answer, she lets something, we don't know what, come and go (is it merely the photo?). Resting one hand on the other's knee, she maintains contact, nothing more. There is no caress, but no distance either. Our bodies touch again, or already touch. They touch one another with their eyes, in any case, bodies that are neither entangled nor disentangled, neither entwined nor unentwined. *We are here*, but we don't add: *we are queer*. Nothing is decided. Maybe we are friends brought together in this particular moment, nothing more. Still, sex is on display here in the two bushes of pubic hair and their double woven into the heavy carpet hanging on the wall—a woolly double that looks like some sort of bat. Like it, we are double: birds and rodents, strange nocturnal animals. How could nudity not be strange? In every instant, everywhere, in the most ordinary course of things and in the banal presence of the body, nudity introduces strangeness. Strangeness invades the skin that is so familiar, so obvious, just as it invades the image in the carpet. But this strangeness is itself familiar. Not every nudity is glorious, just as not every nudity is shameful. With us, there's no shame or modesty, no splendor of the flesh and no suffering. There is no *élan* and no fall. There is neither desire nor sin. There's a suspension: the right angle made by the vertical lines—one woman and the carpet—and the horizontal lines—the other woman and the bed—and the corner of the room that corresponds, diagonally, to the lower right corner of the image, an incongruous and unjustifiable foreground, like an intentional mistake. It's a pile of rough, heavy cloth, like a blanket thrown off the bed and toward the camera, coming a little too close to hitting it. An intentional mistake, or an accident that's been retained: that's the way it is; it's here, there is cloth and skin, an ordinary touch, a crumpling. Banal nudity is undecidable between anguish and abandon. Skin is exposed, unaware of itself, offering itself and holding itself back. It watches itself as we watch ourselves and watch you. One is consciousness, the other unconscious, each one the one of the other, and of you too, you who are naked, like us.

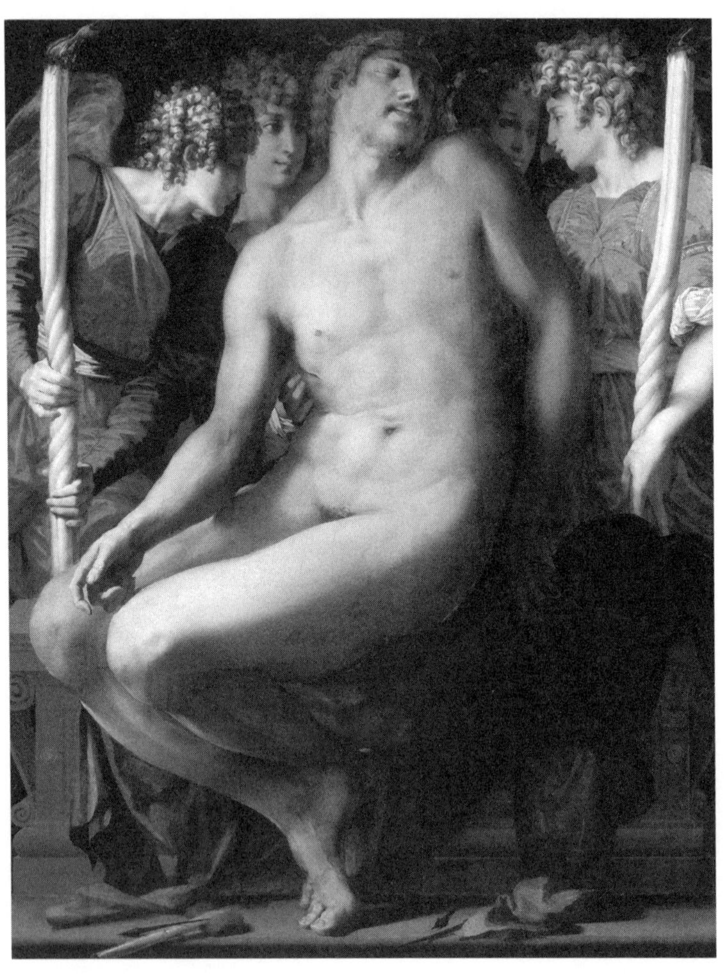

X

I look at him, this dead Christ who seems not so much dead as in ecstasy, beyond himself or in himself for the first time, caught up in his own body in a transport that isn't very mystical but is distinctly sensual. I look at him and wonder what Bishop Leonardo Tournabuoni must have thought when he saw it for the first time, probably sometime around 1527 (before or after the sack of Rome?).[22] This sinuous body is far removed from the iconography of the dead Christ attended by angels, is perhaps closer to the pagan image of Adonis—but is in fact detached from all canonical references (even the formal style, which follows Michelangelo's, is disfigured here by flesh that is too vibrant and sensual, too human). The hairs that appear between the legs of this Christ with such exceptional force, so profoundly real in a composition where reality flees in all directions, where everything seems to surrender to the internal logic of the painting—this skin, stretched out and wholly lacking in mystery, this incarnation without the slightest trace of divinity but simply flesh, a simple body—I wonder what this body must have been back then.[23]

I think of Pier Paolo Pasolini, and the charges of blaspheming against the religion of the state that were brought against him for *Curd Cheese* (La Ricotta), which recreates another Rosso

X

Fiorentino chef d'oeuvre, *Deposition from the Cross*, as a tableau vivant. I think of the words of one of his poems, which Pasolini saw fit to attach to the proceedings of the trial: "Usage and liturgy now profoundly extinct / live on in its style—and in the sun—/ for those who understand its presence and poetry."[24]

Rosso Fiorentino's Dead Christ oscillates between a blasphemous transgression of all canons and a simple exposure to the presence of the body of art, for which all themes are appropriate and whose only rule is the rule given in the act of creating it. Pasolini understood this well, and it is demonstrated by all authentic attempts at nakedness in art.

Christ is now beyond deposition. His position is negated: all the symbols have fallen away—he is completely naked. Rosso has denuded Christ (more out of desire than violence). It is not a matter of transforming this nudity that strips Christ bare in an attempt to expose painting to itself in a new position—as had been the case with certain classical and neoclassical aesthetics that turned to the nude in search of a path to a new truth or essence (the nude as the essence of art). The nakedness of this Christ—but is it still only a Christ?—is the exaltation of a nude not as splendor and the truth of humanity, but as an infinite movement by which nudity is denuded, an infinite passage from *veritatis* splendor to a "liquid splendor of colors" (Pasolini again). The meaning of the nude has to do with this repeated attempt to depose all finite positions that open onto no transcendence or *über*-essence of art—no liturgy, just "style," "presence," and "poetry."

It is the scandal of the nude and the nudity of art, the displacement of its religious aura in favor of its being there, of its silent presence, its "manner," its style, its mere praxis.

The nude—and this nude more so than other nudes—stands enigmatically between two X's: on the one hand, the X of censure, scandal, the X that has fun transgressing thanks to a taste for contradiction, creating a scandal for public opinion and among right-thinking people, wreaking havoc in the midst of the boring papers of the academic world and its lackeys. On the other hand, the unknown, the mathematical variable that cannot be defined, on which no definite identity can be imposed and which, precisely for this reason, surprises you, creates a stupor that is constant but solitary, that is addressed to you and you alone.

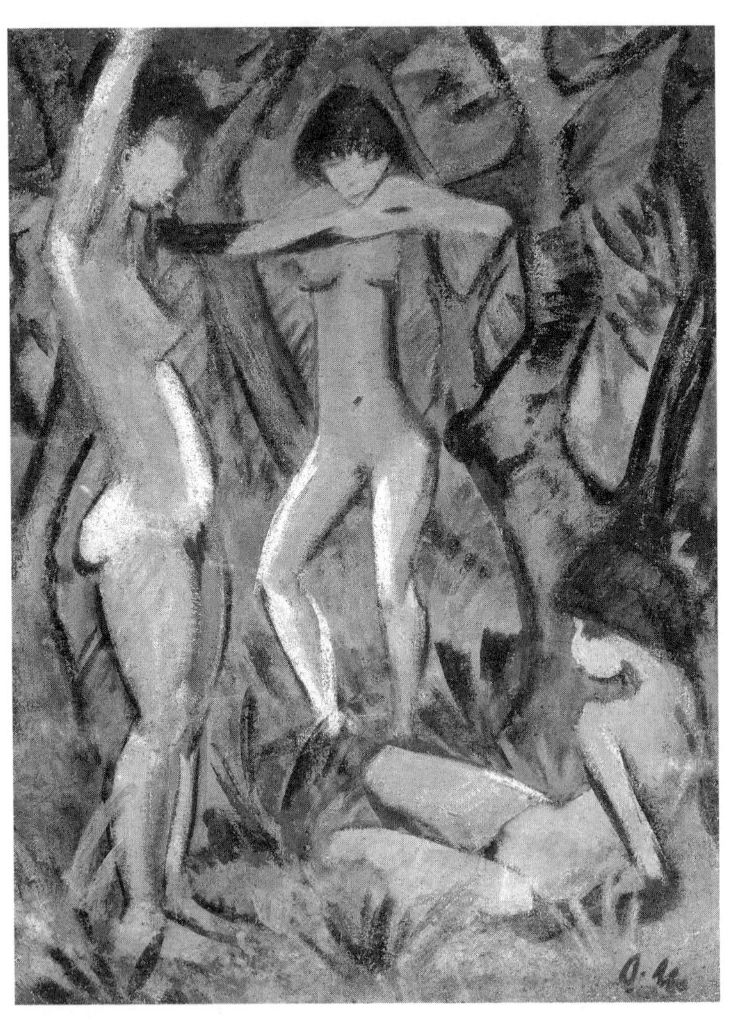

y

The geometrical center of this canvas is situated exactly between the thighs of the central nude, at the bottom extremity of her pubis, right where the dark patch at the bottom of the belly blends into the shadow on the back of the right thigh and into the blurred background where, nevertheless, there gleams a tiny double mark of blue that appears—even though it hardly appears at all—precisely to mark the center. As if it were somehow necessary to underline this median point still more, the interior line of the right thigh, continued along the left side of the groin, leaves no doubt: this is where the diagonal lines of the rectangular frame cross, the second one beginning in the bottom right-hand corner of the picture with the line of an arm. Above the center point are two vertical parallel lines of an elongated torso, which support the pensive head and the overhanging, suspended arms, resting on a branch above the round breasts. Above the vagina, there is a navel that is also dark and clearly set apart, marking with a dot what should have been the center. But in fact this fake center provokes the eye to judge and leads it further down, to the double point of the ascending and descending triangles.

Whatever this triangular head is thinking is the thought around which the three women are immobilized: they themselves, their

y

triple presence, the triangle of their three pubes, the triple fork of their intimate nudity, which is sometimes called "the center of the body." Here the center is not punctuated; it opens and closes constantly on the point of an indefinite number of tree forks, leaves, thighs, and even a breast and a hip. It is easy to see that these nudes are meditating, or are remaining thoughtful in the face of their three nudities, exposed to one another and to the forest that envelops them, sultry and forked. The nude and the triangle communicate by means of a sort of synonymy. The angle of the triangle is acute, incisive; the figure divides the canvas into multiple corners and points, all of them imbricated in each other.

Nudity appears as a cutting of the bodies and of space. It does not bend back on itself. It traces a network of lines that join and part, a network of meetings and spacing. Immobility serves only to throw into relief the ceaseless beat of crossing and recrossing. The triangle is the elementary shape of geometry, the most open one. It does not close like a square or a circle but spreads its sides out beyond its apexes into ever more triangles. The center of the body is not a center but a crossing and spacing. Its crotch both tightens up and stretches out the whole circumscription of a body's exposed skin.

Three women in the woods, and we don't even get to see the stream that might have provided a pretext for bathing. Just three women in a triangle of vegetation: branches, boughs, twigs, shoots, all places of a tender, nervous spacing, bifurcation, equivocation, budding, the rising of the sap. The sunlight penetrates this far, and the bodies are spangled with gold. But the sap seeps here: there's no agitation, but a gathering. The entire trinitarian mythology of the female nude and all of the typologies of femininity as split are powerfully recapitulated here: three Graces, three goddesses judged by Paris, three witches, three *shakti*. It is not that three is feminine but that woman is triangulated. Not unique or coupled or gathered into herself in a square or circle, but always with one extra; each one of the three apexes is excessive and at a distance. At an angle, the nude opens and closes, is prolonged beyond itself and points infinitely toward its excess, its pubescence.

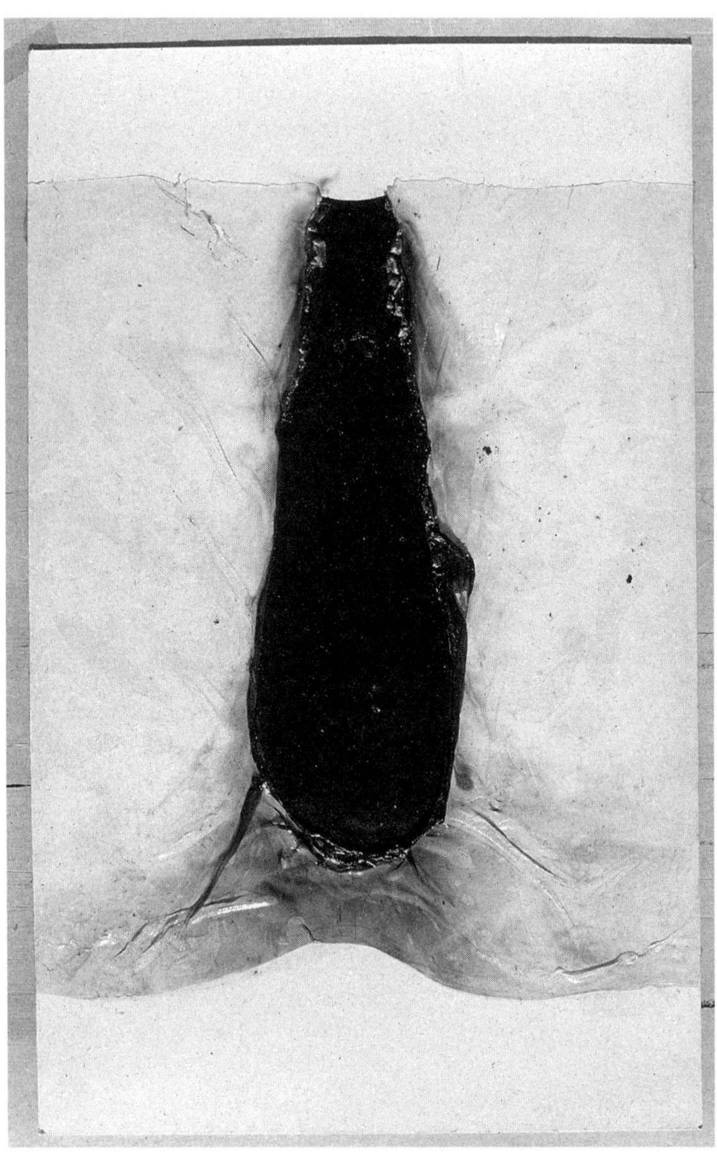

Zero

A combustion of plastic, acrylic, paper, and vinyl on cardboard. Simply a burning, an unexpected mutation of the material, a metamorphosis, the passage from one state to another. Vision is simplified. Everything becomes simple, *sim-plex*. Black and white. Nothing else. "The origin of the world" to which nothing is left but its own *semi*-unformed material. There is no longer any symbolism or allegory, only a passage, but it is not a metaphor. Friction, combustion: the emission of light and heat.

Material presence or chromatic material. Presence beyond the rules of representation and anatomy. ("The painting that has 'a naked man' as its subject is not to be reckoned according to human anatomy but according to the anatomy of painting"; Paul Klee, *Journal*.)[25]

The nude appears starting from a waiting for nothing, a gaze that is laid bare and has no nostalgia for the complaisant solitude of the form. It is the simple waiting of a body that is hidden from its own image, a body that becomes body through the material of the picture, a body that is exposed to its being, its outside, to the fact that it is its own outside. Exposition: stepping out of position, outside what is set in place, and therefore an opening to the negativity of matter, its resistance in the face of all will to representation. The nude flees into the obscurity of the material and into its dazzling luminosity, its candor. It is not only solid matter but also rhythm, wave, curve, oscillation, resonance, dissonance, and consonance between the rough walls of a gorge: *Abgrund*. Before the nothingness of matter, before the black hole into which matter seems to disappear and in which light is lost, the nude appears. It no longer appears as the negative of a given positive, but as the indiscernible point where positivity passes over into negativity and negativity brushes up against positivity. The nude is the zero point of material. Zero: neither positive nor negative. A place without limits where before and beyond all painting, a figure is drawn.

Illustration Sources and Credits

A. Attributed to Franciscus van der Steen, *Jupiter and Antiope* (after Van Dyck, 1655–60). © Trustees of the British Museum.

B. Rembrandt van Rijn, *Bathsheba in the Bath* (1654). Oil on Canvas, 142 × 142 cm. Louvre, Paris, France. Erich Lessing / Art Resource, N.Y.

C. Paul Cézanne, *Afternoon in Naples* (*L'Après-midi à Naples*; ca.1875). National Gallery of Australia, Canberra, purchased 1985.

D. Francis Bacon, *Study for a Nude* (1951). © 2013 The Estate of Francis Bacon. All rights reserved. / ARS, New York / DACS, London.

E. Jacques-Louis David, *Apelles Painting Campaspe* (*Apelle peignant Campaspe*, 1814). Palais des Beaux Arts, Lille, France. © RMN–Grand Palais / Art Resource, N.Y.

F. David Hockney, *Ian Washing His Hair, London, Jan. 1983*. Photographic Collage. 30 × 33". Edition of 15. © David Hockney.

G. Francisco Goya, *The Nude Maja* (*Maja desnuda*, 1797–1800) and *The Clothed Maja* (*Maja vestida*, 1800–8). Museo del Prado, Madrid, Spain. Scala / Art Resource, N.Y.

H. Rembrandt van Rijn, *The Fall of Man* (1638). Etching. Second of two states. Bpk, Berlin / Kupferstichkabinett, Staatliche Museen / Jörg P. Anders / Art Resource, N.Y.

I. Lucian Freud, *Girl with Closed Eyes* (1986–87). Private Collection. © Lucian Freud Archive / Bridgeman Art Library.

J. Annibale Carracci, *The Furious Cyclops Polyphemus Throwing a Rock from the Volcano Etna at Men*, from *Loves of the Gods* frescos (1602), Carracci

Gallery, Palazzo Farnese, Rome, Italy. Gianni Dagli Orti / The Art Archive at Art Resource, N.Y.

K. Anselm Kiefer, *Olympia* (1999). Reproduced by permission of the artist.

L. Cornelisz van Haarlem, *Study of a Man Undressing, Seen from the Back* (1597). Hessisches Landesmuseum Darmstadt. Photo: Wolfgang Fuhrmannek.

M. Eugene Delacroix, *Sitting Nude*, also called *Mlle. Rose* (1820). Louvre, Paris, France. Erich Lessing / Art Resource, N.Y.

N. Giovanni Bellini, *Woman at the Mirror* (*Jeune femme au miroir*, 1515). Kunsthistorisches Museum, Vienna, Austria. Photo credit: Erich Lessing / Art Resource, N.Y.

O. Theresa Murphy, *Self* (2000). © Theresa Murphy.

P. Edward Weston, *Tina on the Azotea* (1924). Collection Center for Creative Photography. ©1981 Arizona Board of Regents.

Q. Jacopo da Pontormo, *Self-portrait in Underpants* (*Autoritratto in mutande*). © Trustees of the British Museum.

R. Giotto di Bondone, *The Last Judgment* (*Le Jugement dernier*, 1303–6, detail). Scrovegni Chapel, Padua, Italy. Cameraphoto Arte, Venice / Art Resource, N.Y.

S. Ugo Mulas, *Pistoletto* (1970). Photo Ugo Mulas. © Ugo Mulas Heirs. All rights reserved.

T. Nan Goldin, *Ryan in the Tub* (1976).

U. Daniel Julien, *Peep Show* (1997). Reproduced by permission of the artist.

V. Sandro Botticelli, *Truth*, détail of *The Calumny of Apelles* (ca. 1494). Galleria degli Uffizi Florence. Gianni Dagli Orti / The Art Archive at Art Resource, N.Y.

W. Nikolay Bakharev, *Untitled* (2000). Grinberg Gallery.

X. Rosso Fiorentino, *The Dead Christ with Angels* (1524–27). Boston Museum of Fine Arts.

Y. Otto Müller, *Three Nude Figures in the Wood* (1911). Sprengel Museum, Hannover, Germany. © DeA Picture Library / Art Resource, N.Y.

Z. Alberto Burri, *Combustione* (1964). Carta, plastic, acrilico, vinavil, ombustione su cartoncino, 56 × 35.6 cm. © Fondazione Palazzo Albizzini Collezione Burri, Città di Castello—by SIAE 2013, © 2013 Artists Rights Society (ARS), N.Y.

124

Notes

1. Friedrich Nietzsche, *The Gay Science*, trans. Walter Kaufmann (New York: Vintage, 1974), 295.

2. Kenneth Clark, *The Nude: A Study in Ideal Form* (Princeton, N.J.: Princeton University Press, 1956); Erwin Panofsky, Studies in Iconology: Humanistic Themes in the Art of the Renaissance (New York: Harper, 1967).

3. François Jullien, *De l'essence ou du nu—Avec des photographies de Ralph Gibson* (Paris: Seuil, 2000), 69.

4. See Hans Jantzen, *Rembrandt* (Bielefeld: Velhagen and Klasing, 1923).

5. Cézanne did another painting with the same title, which was later owned by Lucian Freud, who himself did a painting on the same subject (National Gallery of Australia, Canberra).

6. The complete title is: Eadweard Muybridge, *Animal Locomotion. An Electro-Photographic Investigation of Consecutive Phases of Animal Movements* (1887).

7. This hypothesis is analyzed with great historical and theoretical finesse by Svetlana Alpers in *The Art of Describing: Dutch Art in the Seventeenth Century* (Chicago: University of Chicago Press, 1983), and more recently by Victor I. Stoichita, in *L'instauration du tableau* (Paris: Klinck-sieck, 1993).

8. Roland Barthes, *La chambre claire* (Paris: Cahiers du cinéma, 1980), 28.

9. Leon Battista Alberti, *Della pittura* (Florence: Sansoni, 1950).

10. The two *Majas*, by contrast, are life size.

11. One could compare these violent scenes with the two "Cannibalistic Scenes" at Besançon. In one of them, a woman takes part in eating the flesh of a man who has been ripped to pieces.

12. Michel Deguy, "D'une physique erotique," *L'Arc*, no. 32 (1967), rpt.Paris : Duponchelle, 1990.

13. Picasso remarked that the sun and the erect penis are the two aporias of painting. See J. M. Pontévia, *La peinture, masque et miroir* (Bordeaux: William Blake & Co., 1993), 1:29.

14. The painting is composed following canto 4 of Ovid's *Metamorphoses*. It is worth remembering that elsewhere (e.g., in *The Child Hercules* or *Hercules Between Vice and Virtue*, as in certain other drawings), Annibale Carracci was happy to put the penis in the center of the composition. Moreover, it is possible that his brother Agostino, who was the author of, among other things, a famous series of erotic engravings illustrating the Aretino, helped him with this fresco of Polyphemus.

15. Martin Heidegger, *Nietzsche*, trans. David Farrell Krell (San Francisco: Harper and Row, 1984), 2:91.

16. See, e.g., Roberto Longhi, *Breve ma veridica storia della pittura italiana* (Milan: Rizzoli, 1999).

17. Rainer Maria Rilke, *Die Weise von Liebe und Tod des Cornets Christoph Rilke* (Frankfurt am Main: Suhrkamp, 1996).

18. See Patrick Baudry, *La pornographie et ses images* (Paris: Armand Colin, 1997), "Seeing Oneself Seeing," 224: "The film X should certainly be considered a monstration but also a demonstration. It is not only an exhibition but is a supervision of this exhibition."

19. [The Marquis de Sade, Philosophy in the Bedroom, dialogue 5, in *The Complete Justine, Philosophy in the Bedroom, and Other Writings*, trans. Richard Seaver and Austryn Wainhouse (New York: Grove Press, 1965), 281.—Trans.]

126

20. Apropos the genesis of this painting, Aby Warburg's theses developed in *"La Naissance de Vénus"* and *"Le Printemps de Sandro Botticelli,"* in *Essais florentins* (Paris: Klincksieck, 1990) are still valuable, as well as the work of Edgar Wind, *Mystères païens à la Renaissance* (Paris: Gallimard, 1992); see also Georges Didi-Huberman's *Ouvrir Vénus: Nudité, rêve, cruauté* (Paris: Gallimard, 1999).

21. [In English in the original.—Trans.]

22. Leonardo Tournabuoni was born in 1494, like Rosso Fiorentino, and when he was only twenty-eight years old he was named bishop of San Sepolcro by Pope Hadrian VI, the former imperial preceptor who was close to Erasmus of Rotterdam. He soon made a reputation for himself as a reformer of the church. It is thought that he was close to the order of the *Théatins* and congregation of *Divin Amour*, to which men such as Bembo and Castiglione belonged. It is uncertain where the *Dead Christ* that Rosso Fiorentino was commissioned to paint was destined to go: maybe it was for personal devotion or for a private oratory or even for the mortuary chapel of Tournabuoni himself. After the pillage of Rome, as Vasari recounts, Rosso Fiorentino turned up at San Sepolcro to find his friend Tournabuoni: the two men were thirty-three years old. There is no doubt that on this occasion they found themselves before the *Dead Christ* for the first time. Regarding this, see David Franklin, *Rosso in Italy: The Italian Career of Rosso Fiorentino* (New Haven, Conn.: Yale University Press, 1994). Franklin thinks that the painting was not yet finished at the time of the pillage of Rome. See also P. Costamagna, *"La creation de l'ordre des Théatins et ses repercussions sur l'art de Rosso Fiorentino et de ses contemporains,"* in *Pontormo e Rosso*, ed. R. P. Ciardi and A. Natali (Venice: Marsilio, 1996), 157–63.

23. The only symbols that refer us to the dimension of the divine are the torches of eternal light on the sides and the instruments of the Passion thrown at the feet of Christ, on the stone ground (J. Shearman, "The Dead Christ, by Rosso Fiorentino," *Boston Museum Bulletin* 64, 338 [1966]: 148–72).

24. Pier Paolo Pasolini, "Poems Around Town" (June 10, 1962), trans. N. S. Thompson, *Poetry Nation Review* 202 (November/December 2011): 52.

25. Cited by Pierre Klossowski in *La resemblance* (Marseilles: *Ryôan-ji*, 1984). 62.